Mandates, Motors, and Misinformation

John Shenton

Published by John Shenton, 2024.

While every precaution has been taken in the preparation of this book, the publisher assumes no responsibility for errors or omissions, or for damages resulting from the use of the information contained herein.

MANDATES, MOTORS, AND MISINFORMATION

First edition. September 25, 2024.

ISBN: 979-8227356987

Written by John Shenton.

Also by John Shenton

Business Plan Basics

The Bahamas - More Islands and Recipes Than You Expect!

Collected Musings from Bricks and Mortar to E-commerce

The Smart City Odyssey: Unveiling the Secrets to Traveller-Centric Software

The Dragon's Gambit: China's Bid for Global Dominance and the Western Response

Silent Weapon

Business Basics: Money Sources

Influx

Fried Chips

Mandates, Motors, and Misinformation

Echos of Orwell

Control and Chaos

The Empire's Warning: What Rome's Fall Tells Us About the West Today

Table of Contents

Foreword

In an era marked by rapid technological advancement and ambitious visions of the future, we find ourselves at a crossroads where our cities, our vehicles, and our very ways of life are being reimagined. The concept of "smart cities" has captivated the imagination of urban planners, policymakers, and tech giants alike, promising a seamless integration of technology and daily living. Electric vehicles (EVs) are heralded as the silver bullet for our environmental woes, a symbol of progress on wheels. Yet, beneath the surface of these grand promises lies a more complicated, less discussed reality—one fraught with logistical challenges, unintended consequences, and yes, even misinformation.

This book, *"Mandates, Motors, and Misinformation: A Critical Look at Urban Futures,"* is not just a collection of opinions but a necessary exploration of the assumptions that underpin our drive toward a "smarter" world. As someone who has spent years observing, participating in, and sometimes challenging these narratives, I've seen firsthand how easily optimism can outpace practicality, and how well-intentioned policies can sometimes lead us down paths that are neither sustainable nor equitable.

Smart cities are often presented as the ultimate solution for urban living—cities that are more efficient, more sustainable, and more responsive to the needs of their citizens. But we must ask: at what cost? Are these cities truly being designed for the people who live in them, or for the companies that stand to profit from them? Are we building urban utopias, or are we inadvertently creating digital dystopias where data is the new currency, and privacy becomes a luxury?

Similarly, the push for electric vehicles brings its own set of promises and pitfalls. While EVs are undeniably a critical step toward reducing carbon emissions, the reality of their widespread adoption raises serious questions. Is our electrical grid, already strained in many regions, capable of supporting a mass transition to electric mobility?

What about the environmental and geopolitical consequences of battery production, reliant as it is on rare earth minerals? And who ultimately bears the cost of these transitions—the consumers, the taxpayers, or the corporations?

Government mandates, too, often reflect a top-down approach that lacks the nuance and flexibility required for real-world application. Policies meant to drive change can sometimes clash with the very market forces and consumer behaviours they aim to influence. The result is often a patchwork of solutions that fail to address the root problems or, worse, create new ones. This book does not claim to have all the answers, but it does ask the questions that many seem reluctant to consider.

The chapters that follow will guide you through these complex issues, providing not just critiques but also alternatives. We will explore the potential and pitfalls of current urban and transportation strategies, shining a light on both the successes and the shortcomings. This book is a call for a more thoughtful approach—one that balances innovation with practicality, sustainability with affordability, and ambition with humility.

As you read through these pages, I encourage you to consider the broader context of the narratives being sold to us. Who benefits from these visions of the future? Who might be left behind? And most importantly, how can we, as citizens, consumers, and policymakers, shape a future that is not just smart, but wise?

Welcome to a critical conversation on the future of our cities, our vehicles, and our world.

John Shenton

Part I: The Vision of Smart Cities and Their Discontents

Smart Cities: A Blueprint for the Future or a Fantasy?

The concept of "smart cities" has captivated urban planners, technology enthusiasts, and policymakers alike. Promising to revolutionize the way cities function, smart cities are often portrayed as the solution to the myriad problems facing urban areas today—traffic congestion, energy inefficiency, waste management, pollution, and crime. But as with any ambitious vision, the idea of smart cities is fraught with both potential and pitfalls. Are smart cities a realistic blueprint for the future, or are they an overly idealistic fantasy that fails to account for real-world complexities?

What Are Smart Cities?

A smart city leverages information and communication technology (ICT) to enhance the quality and performance of urban services such as energy, transportation, and utilities, to reduce resource consumption, waste, and overall costs. The goal is to improve the quality of life for citizens through the use of technology. Think of smart traffic lights that adapt in real-time to traffic conditions, public transportation systems that predict demand and adjust routes accordingly, or waste management systems that optimize collection schedules based on the fill levels of bins.

A fully realized smart city would integrate various IoT (Internet of Things) devices, sensors, and data analytics to create a more responsive and efficient urban environment. Smart cities also rely on citizen engagement through mobile applications and platforms where residents can report issues, access city services, and stay informed about municipal affairs.

The Ambitious Vision Behind Smart Cities

The driving force behind smart cities is the ambition to make urban environments more livable, sustainable, and resilient. With rapid urbanization—over 68% of the global population is projected to live in urban areas by 2050—cities face increasing pressure to provide basic services efficiently. Smart city initiatives promise to optimize resource use, reduce energy consumption, and improve the overall well-being of citizens.

Key areas where smart city technologies are expected to bring about transformative change include:

1. **Transportation and Mobility:** Intelligent transportation systems (ITS) that utilize AI and machine learning can reduce traffic congestion, lower emissions, and enhance public safety. Autonomous vehicles, smart traffic signals, and real-time public transport data can create seamless, multi-modal transportation networks.

2. **Energy Management:** Smart grids and smart meters allow for more efficient energy use, integrating renewable energy sources and providing real-time data to consumers and utility providers. This can help in managing peak loads, reducing waste, and lowering carbon footprints.

3. **Public Safety and Security:** Using data analytics and predictive policing, smart cities aim to enhance public safety by anticipating and mitigating crime. Surveillance systems, facial recognition, and AI-driven analysis can assist in rapid response to emergencies.

4. **Healthcare and Education:** Telemedicine and smart health monitoring can make healthcare more accessible, especially in

underserved areas. Similarly, digital education platforms can provide quality education to more people, regardless of their geographic location.

5. **Environmental Sustainability:** From smart water management systems to pollution sensors and green building technologies, smart cities aim to tackle environmental challenges head-on. The integration of these systems allows for more sustainable and eco-friendly urban living.

The Challenges and Realities of Building Smart Cities

While the vision of smart cities is undeniably appealing, the path to achieving this vision is strewn with challenges. For many cities, especially in developing nations, these challenges may make the concept of a fully integrated smart city appear more like a fantasy than a feasible reality.

1. **High Costs and Investment Requirements:** Developing a smart city requires significant investment in infrastructure, technology, and talent. For cities already grappling with financial constraints, such investments may not be justifiable or sustainable.

2. **Data Privacy and Security Concerns:** The deployment of vast networks of sensors and cameras raises substantial concerns about data privacy and surveillance. Citizens may be wary of living in cities where their every move is monitored and data is collected by both government and private entities. There are also risks of cyberattacks and data breaches, which could have catastrophic effects on a city's operations.

3. **Digital Divide and Inclusivity Issues:** Not all citizens have equal access to digital technology, and not all are equally comfortable using it. There is a risk that smart city initiatives could inadvertently widen the gap between those who are

digitally literate and those who are not, marginalizing certain segments of the population.

4. **Complex Integration and Interoperability:** Building a smart city requires the seamless integration of numerous technologies, platforms, and stakeholders. Achieving interoperability among different systems and ensuring they work cohesively is a monumental challenge.

5. **Dependence on Technology and Its Implications:** The more a city depends on technology, the more vulnerable it becomes to failures, whether through technical glitches, cyber-attacks, or power outages. A truly smart city must be resilient, but building this resilience into technological systems is no easy feat.

6. **Ethical and Governance Concerns:** Who controls the data in a smart city? Who decides what technology to deploy and where? These questions raise ethical concerns around governance, accountability, and citizen rights. A smart city without transparent, inclusive, and participatory governance could lead to a dystopian scenario rather than a utopian one.

Case Studies: The Promise and Perils of Smart City Initiatives

Several cities around the world have embarked on the journey to becoming "smart." For example, **Barcelona**, Spain, is often cited as a leading example. The city has implemented smart street lighting, waste management, and even a smart water management system, all of which have contributed to cost savings and improved services. Similarly, **Singapore** is leveraging technology for urban mobility, environmental sustainability, and public safety, making it one of the most advanced smart cities globally.

However, not all smart city initiatives have been successful. **Songdo**, South Korea, envisioned as the world's first fully functional smart city, has faced challenges in attracting residents and businesses. The high costs and lack of social infrastructure have led some critics to label it as a "ghost city." This illustrates that technology alone cannot create a vibrant urban environment; social, cultural, and economic factors are equally crucial.

The Middle Ground: Pragmatic Steps Towards Smarter Cities

Given the challenges, it might be more pragmatic to think of "smarter cities" rather than fully-fledged smart cities. Incremental advancements in technology, better urban planning, and improved citizen engagement can still yield significant benefits. Instead of attempting to build smart cities from scratch, existing cities can adopt smart solutions in targeted areas where they have the most impact.

1. **Prioritize Local Needs:** Different cities have different challenges. Urban planners should focus on deploying technologies that address their specific issues, whether it is traffic congestion, waste management, or public safety.

2. **Promote Public-Private Partnerships:** Collaboration between governments, businesses, and citizens is crucial for the successful implementation of smart city initiatives. Public-private partnerships can provide the necessary funding, expertise, and innovation to drive smart city projects.

3. **Ensure Inclusivity and Equity:** Smart city initiatives should be designed to be inclusive, ensuring that all residents—regardless of socioeconomic status—benefit from technological advancements.

4. **Focus on Resilience:** Urban resilience must be built into the very fabric of smart cities. This means preparing for the unexpected, whether it be cyberattacks, natural disasters, or

system failures.

Conclusion: Blueprint for the Future or a Fantasy?

Smart cities represent a powerful vision of the future of urban living, one that combines technology, sustainability, and improved quality of life. However, this vision must be tempered with realism. While technology can undoubtedly address many of the challenges facing cities today, it is not a panacea. For smart cities to become a reality, they must be built on a foundation of sound urban planning, ethical governance, inclusivity, and citizen engagement. In essence, smart cities are both a blueprint for the future and, in some respects, a fantasy—but one that, with careful planning and execution, could inch closer to reality.

Urban Utopias or Digital Nightmares? Examining the Potential Risks and Unintended Consequences of Hyper-Connected Cities and Digital Currencies

The promise of "smart cities" powered by hyper-connected technology is one that many urban planners and technologists envision as a utopia. These cities, leveraging the Internet of Things (IoT), artificial intelligence (AI), big data, and even digital currencies, are imagined as spaces where efficiency, sustainability, and safety reign supreme. From smart grids that manage energy use to autonomous vehicles that eliminate traffic jams, the future of urban living appears to be brighter than ever. However, beneath this utopian vision lies a complex web of potential risks and unintended consequences. As we stand on the precipice of this digital transformation, it is vital to ask: Are we truly building urban utopias, or are we creating digital nightmares where privacy, freedom, and autonomy are compromised?

The Erosion of Privacy and the Specter of Surveillance

Smart cities promise an unprecedented level of efficiency by using real-time data to manage urban infrastructure, from traffic lights to waste management. However, the cost of this efficiency often comes at the expense of privacy. The infrastructure of smart cities relies on a vast network of sensors, cameras, and data-collection devices that monitor nearly every aspect of urban life. While these systems can enhance public safety and service delivery, they also create a pervasive surveillance environment where every movement, interaction, and transaction can be tracked and analyzed.

The promise that data will be anonymized and used ethically is not enough to mitigate the risks of misuse. In an environment where every action is monitored, there is an ever-present danger of "surveillance creep," where data collected for seemingly benign purposes—like improving traffic flow—could be repurposed for more invasive monitoring. This surveillance can easily extend beyond public spaces and seep into private lives, eroding the distinction between what is public and what is private. The potential misuse of this data by both state and non-state actors is alarming, ranging from targeted advertising and social profiling to more sinister uses like political repression and social control.

The Fragility of Digital Dependency and the Rise of Digital Currencies

As cities become more dependent on digital infrastructure, they also become more vulnerable to its failure. A hyper-connected city relies on technology to function smoothly. What happens when that technology fails? Cyber-attacks, system malfunctions, or even natural disasters could bring a smart city to its knees, disrupting everything from emergency services to water supply. The potential for chaos in such scenarios is not just theoretical; it is a likely outcome in a world where digital systems manage essential services.

This digital dependency becomes even more concerning with the introduction of government-proposed digital currencies, often referred to as Central Bank Digital Currencies (CBDCs). While digital currencies are touted as a way to streamline transactions, reduce costs, and combat illegal activities, they also introduce a new layer of control and surveillance. Unlike cash, which provides a certain level of anonymity, digital currencies can be programmed, monitored, and controlled by central authorities. This creates an opportunity for governments to track every transaction made by a citizen, effectively eliminating financial privacy.

The ability to program digital currencies could also lead to unprecedented forms of control. Imagine a situation where a government decides that certain activities are undesirable—like buying specific types of goods, funding protests, or even donating to political causes. With digital currencies, it would be relatively straightforward to restrict or block transactions that do not align with government policies. The potential for such misuse is vast, and it poses a significant threat to individual freedoms and democratic governance.

Algorithmic Governance, Social Inequality, and Economic Control

The integration of AI and machine learning into smart city governance is seen as a way to optimize urban management, from law enforcement to resource allocation. However, this algorithmic approach can perpetuate or even worsen existing social inequalities. Many predictive systems used in smart cities are based on data that reflects historical biases. For example, predictive policing algorithms might target certain communities more aggressively based on past crime data, creating a self-reinforcing cycle of over-policing and distrust.

The introduction of digital currencies further complicates this landscape. These currencies could enable new forms of economic control that exacerbate inequality. For example, digital currencies could be used to implement "social credit" systems that reward or punish citizens based on their behaviour, affecting everything from access to credit to eligibility for public services. Such systems would likely disadvantage marginalized communities that are already at risk of systemic bias and discrimination.

The Threat of Corporate Control and Digital Colonialism

While the narrative around smart cities often focuses on citizen empowerment, the reality is that many of these projects are driven by technology companies eager to profit from lucrative contracts and partnerships with city governments. This dynamic can lead to a form of digital colonialism where cities become testbeds for new technologies, often without the full consent or understanding of their residents.

Digital currencies could play a role in this process by facilitating the monetization of urban data and services. Tech companies could leverage digital currencies to create closed ecosystems where transactions, data, and services are all controlled within a proprietary network. This could lead to a privatization of public spaces and services, turning citizens into mere consumers subject to the terms and conditions set by corporations.

Homogenized Urban Experiences and the Loss of Freedom

The push for smart cities and digital currencies risks creating environments that prioritize efficiency and control over diversity, spontaneity, and freedom. Cities have traditionally been spaces of diversity, where different cultures, ideas, and lifestyles come together. However, in a highly managed, algorithm-driven city, there is a risk that urban life becomes homogenized and sterile. When algorithms dictate everything from traffic flows to which businesses can operate in certain areas, we lose the organic, messy, and unpredictable nature of cities that makes them vibrant and human.

Similarly, digital currencies, while convenient, could impose new forms of financial control that limit individual freedom. In a world where every transaction is traceable and controllable, the ability to act freely—whether that means supporting a political cause, starting a controversial business, or simply living without constant oversight—becomes compromised.

Conclusion: Navigating the Future with Caution

The vision of smart cities powered by hyper-connected technology and digital currencies is compelling, but it comes with significant risks that must be carefully navigated. While the potential benefits are real—enhanced efficiency, sustainability, and safety—the potential for misuse is equally significant. Privacy, security, equity, and freedom must be at the core of any smart city and digital currency initiative. Otherwise, we risk building cities that serve as digital cages rather than thriving human habitats.

As we move towards a future of interconnected cities and digital currencies, we must ensure that technology is used to enhance, rather than constrain, human potential. The challenge is not just to build smarter cities but to build fairer, more inclusive, and more humane cities that respect the rights, freedoms, and diversity of all their inhabitants. Only then can we avoid turning our urban dreams into digital nightmares.

Who Benefits? The Politics and Economics of Smart Urban Planning

Smart cities, with their promise of technological innovation and enhanced quality of life, have become a focal point of contemporary urban planning. These initiatives, leveraging advanced technologies like the Internet of Things (IoT), big data analytics, artificial intelligence (AI), and 5G networks, aim to address urban challenges such as traffic congestion, energy efficiency, waste management, and public safety. However, the politics and economics behind smart urban planning reveal a more complex picture, raising essential questions about who truly benefits from these initiatives and who may be left behind. This article delves into the economic dynamics and political implications of smart city projects, highlighting the interests at play and the potential for inequality in this high-tech urban future.

The Economics of Smart City Initiatives

At their core, smart city projects are massive undertakings that require substantial investment in infrastructure, technology, and governance frameworks. These projects are often positioned as public-private partnerships, where governments collaborate with tech giants, real estate developers, and infrastructure companies to design and implement "smart" solutions for urban environments.

1. Corporate Interests and Profit Motives

One of the driving forces behind smart city initiatives is the profit potential. Large technology firms such as IBM, Cisco, Google, and Siemens, alongside smaller tech startups, see smart cities as lucrative markets for their products and services. These companies offer integrated solutions—ranging from smart grids and traffic management systems to digital surveillance and data analytics platforms—that promise to revolutionize urban living.

While these technologies undoubtedly offer efficiencies and conveniences, they are also profit-driven. The contracts awarded for the design, implementation, and maintenance of smart city technologies can run into billions of dollars, providing a steady stream of revenue for these corporations. This raises the question of whether smart city planning is more about meeting the needs of urban residents or serving the bottom lines of tech companies. When profit motives take precedence, there is a risk that smart city developments may prioritize technological solutions over more sustainable, human-centred urban planning.

2. Real Estate and Property Development

Another key beneficiary of smart urban planning is the real estate sector. Smart city initiatives often involve significant redevelopment of urban areas, transforming them into high-tech hubs that are marketed as safe, efficient, and sustainable. This "smart" branding can significantly increase property values, benefiting real estate developers and property owners.

However, this surge in property values can have a darker side: gentrification. When urban areas are upgraded with smart technology, they often attract higher-income residents and businesses, driving up costs and displacing lower-income communities. This can exacerbate existing social inequalities, leading to a scenario where the wealthy benefit from the smart city boom while marginalized populations are pushed out or left behind.

3. Municipal Governments and Fiscal Benefits

Municipal governments also stand to gain from smart city projects, albeit in different ways. Smart technologies can potentially help cities optimize their resource management, reduce operational costs, and enhance service delivery. For example, smart water and energy grids can reduce waste and cut costs, while predictive policing and digital surveillance can enhance public safety and reduce crime rates. These efficiencies can result in significant savings for city budgets, allowing municipalities to reallocate resources to other critical areas.

Moreover, by partnering with private corporations, cities can leverage private capital to finance these projects, reducing the immediate fiscal burden on taxpayers. However, this raises concerns about the loss of public control over essential urban services. When private entities play a significant role in managing urban infrastructure, there is a risk of prioritizing profit over public welfare, leading to potential conflicts of interest and reduced accountability.

The Politics of Smart Urban Planning

The politics behind smart city initiatives are as significant as the economics. The planning, implementation, and governance of smart cities are deeply political processes that reflect power dynamics, decision-making structures, and competing interests.

1. Governance and Decision-Making

Smart city projects require robust governance frameworks to oversee the integration of technology into urban infrastructure. However, the decision-making processes that guide smart urban planning are often opaque and dominated by a small group of stakeholders—primarily government officials, corporate executives, and technical experts. This exclusionary approach can lead to a lack of public engagement and participation, raising concerns about transparency and accountability.

When citizens are excluded from the decision-making process, there is a risk that smart city projects will not reflect the needs and priorities of the broader community. Instead, they may cater to the interests of a select few—those who stand to benefit financially or politically. This can result in a top-down approach to urban planning, where technology is imposed upon citizens rather than co-created with them.

2. Surveillance and Control

The integration of surveillance technologies into smart city infrastructure is another area where politics comes into play. While these technologies can enhance public safety and security, they also raise concerns about privacy and civil liberties. The deployment of facial recognition cameras, digital tracking systems, and predictive policing algorithms can create environments of pervasive surveillance, where citizens' movements and behaviours are continuously monitored.

This level of surveillance can have a chilling effect on public life, leading to a reduction in freedom of expression, assembly, and association. Moreover, the data collected through these surveillance systems can be used to profile and discriminate against marginalized groups, reinforcing existing social inequalities. The political implications of such surveillance are profound, raising questions about the balance between security and civil rights in smart cities.

3. Who is Left Behind? The Inequities of Smart Cities

While the economic and political benefits of smart cities are apparent for corporations, developers, and some segments of society, the question remains: Who is left behind? The reality is that smart city initiatives can create or exacerbate inequalities in several ways.

Firstly, the digital divide remains a significant barrier to equitable access to smart city benefits. Not all citizens have the same access to digital technologies or the digital literacy required to navigate smart city services. Low-income residents, elderly populations, and those with disabilities may find themselves excluded from the benefits of smart city innovations.

Secondly, the costs associated with living in smart urban environments may increase. As property values rise and the cost of smart services is passed on to consumers, lower-income residents may struggle to keep up with the rising cost of living, potentially leading to displacement and further entrenchment of socio-economic divides.

Lastly, the prioritization of technology-driven solutions can divert attention away from more pressing social issues such as affordable housing, public health, and social equity. When urban planning focuses too heavily on "smart" solutions, it risks neglecting the fundamental needs of its most vulnerable populations.

Toward More Equitable Smart Urban Planning

To ensure that smart cities are truly beneficial for all, it is essential to adopt a more inclusive, transparent, and equitable approach to urban planning. Several key principles can guide this effort:

1. **Inclusive Decision-Making:** Urban planning should involve meaningful participation from a diverse range of stakeholders, including marginalized communities, civil society organizations, and everyday citizens. Public consultations, participatory design processes, and community engagement are crucial to ensuring that smart city initiatives reflect the needs and priorities of all residents.

2. **Equity-Focused Policies:** Smart city projects should prioritize equity by addressing the digital divide, ensuring affordable access to smart services, and preventing the displacement of low-income communities. Policies that focus on social housing, digital literacy programs, and affordable access to smart technologies can help bridge gaps.

3. **Accountable Governance:** Transparency and accountability should be at the heart of smart city governance. Clear regulations governing data privacy, surveillance, and the use of technology are essential to prevent abuses of power and protect civil liberties. Mechanisms for public oversight and independent audits can help ensure that smart city initiatives remain aligned with public interests.

4. **Human-Centred Design:** Rather than being driven solely by technological solutions, smart city planning should prioritize human-centred design that addresses social, cultural, and economic needs. This means focusing on policies that improve overall quality of life, from affordable housing and public transportation to access to education and healthcare.

Conclusion

Smart city initiatives present both opportunities and challenges in the realm of urban planning. While there are significant economic and political interests at play, the benefits of smart cities should not be limited to a select few. By adopting a more inclusive and equitable approach to smart urban planning, cities can ensure that technological advancements serve the broader public good, creating urban environments that are not only smart but also just, sustainable, and humane.

The Data Delusion: Privacy, Surveillance, and Control in Smart Cities

As cities around the world embrace digital transformation, the concept of "smart cities" has evolved from an idealized vision to a tangible reality. With promises of enhanced urban efficiency, sustainability, and quality of life, smart cities leverage data-driven technologies such as the Internet of Things (IoT), artificial intelligence (AI), and big data analytics to optimize everything from traffic management to public safety. However, as these cities become increasingly interconnected and data-dependent, concerns about privacy, surveillance, and control have surged to the forefront of public discourse. The data delusion—the belief that more data automatically leads to better outcomes—presents significant ethical, social, and political challenges that must be addressed to prevent smart cities from becoming surveillance dystopias.

The Promises and Pitfalls of Smart Cities

Smart cities are built on the premise that data is a valuable resource that can be harnessed to make urban environments more livable, efficient, and sustainable. Sensors embedded in streets, buildings, and infrastructure gather vast amounts of data on everything from air quality to pedestrian movement. AI algorithms analyze this data in real-time to optimize services such as public transportation, waste management, and energy distribution. Citizens are promised reduced traffic congestion, faster emergency response times, and a more sustainable urban environment.

While these benefits are enticing, they come with significant trade-offs. The very technologies that enable smart cities to function—such as facial recognition, predictive policing, and automated decision-making systems—can also be used for mass surveillance and social control. The data collected can reveal intimate details about citizens' daily lives, raising serious concerns about privacy, consent, and the potential misuse of information by both public and private entities.

The Surveillance Infrastructure: A Double-Edged Sword

One of the most concerning aspects of smart cities is the pervasive surveillance infrastructure that underpins them. Closed-circuit television (CCTV) cameras, drones, and sensors capable of tracking every movement within the city are often touted as tools for public safety and crime prevention. However, these tools can easily be repurposed for mass surveillance, social profiling, and discrimination.

For example, facial recognition technology has been deployed in cities worldwide to monitor public spaces, identify individuals, and even predict criminal behaviour. While such technology can enhance law enforcement capabilities, it is not without its flaws. Facial recognition systems have been criticized for their inaccuracies, particularly in identifying people of colour, women, and younger individuals. This leads to biased policing practices and potential violations of civil liberties.

Furthermore, smart city technologies often rely on predictive algorithms that analyze data to forecast criminal activity or identify "high-risk" individuals. These algorithms are not immune to bias, as they often reflect the prejudices embedded in the data they are trained on. As a result, marginalized communities can be disproportionately targeted, perpetuating existing inequalities and eroding trust between citizens and authorities.

The Illusion of Consent and the Erosion of Privacy

Another critical concern in smart cities is the illusion of consent. In many cases, citizens are unaware of the extent to which their data is being collected, shared, and analyzed. While city authorities may argue that data collection is necessary for providing efficient services, the lack of transparency and informed consent undermines citizens' autonomy and privacy.

Moreover, the data collected in smart cities is often not anonymized or de-identified, making it possible to trace it back to individual citizens. Even when data is anonymized, advanced data analytics and machine learning techniques can often re-identify individuals, particularly when multiple datasets are combined. This raises the question: who owns the data generated by citizens, and how is it being used?

Private companies that partner with city governments to provide smart city solutions often have access to vast amounts of sensitive data. In many cases, these companies operate with minimal oversight, raising concerns about data breaches, unauthorized data sharing, and potential misuse. The Cambridge Analytica scandal is a stark reminder of how data can be weaponized for political manipulation and control. In smart cities, the stakes are even higher, as the data collected can reveal not just political preferences, but also movement patterns, health conditions, and social behaviours.

The Threat of Data Monopolies and the Commodification of Urban Life

The push towards smart cities has also led to the emergence of data monopolies, where a handful of tech giants control vast amounts of urban data. These companies often operate with little to no accountability, leading to a concentration of power that can undermine democratic governance and citizen rights. The commodification of urban life—where every aspect of a citizen's behaviour can be tracked, analyzed, and monetized—poses a significant threat to individual freedom and social equity.

Furthermore, the data-driven logic of smart cities tends to prioritize efficiency and control over democratic participation and human rights. The focus on data as a tool for governance risks reducing citizens to mere data points, stripping away the complexities of human experience and undermining the democratic values that should underpin urban life.

Balancing Innovation with Privacy: A Call for Ethical Governance

To navigate the data delusion and ensure that smart cities serve the public good, it is essential to establish robust ethical frameworks and governance models. This begins with transparency and accountability. Cities must be transparent about what data is being collected, how it is used, and who has access to it. Citizens should have a say in these processes, and there must be clear mechanisms for oversight and redress in case of misuse.

Additionally, smart cities should prioritize data minimization and privacy by design. This means collecting only the data that is strictly necessary for specific purposes, ensuring that data is anonymized and encrypted, and adopting privacy-preserving technologies such as differential privacy and federated learning. Moreover, smart city initiatives should be guided by principles of social equity, ensuring that marginalized communities are not disproportionately surveilled or excluded from decision-making processes.

Finally, it is crucial to foster a culture of digital literacy and awareness among citizens. People need to understand the implications of data collection and the trade-offs involved in smart city initiatives. By empowering citizens with knowledge and involving them in governance, we can strike a balance between leveraging technology for urban innovation and safeguarding privacy, civil liberties, and human rights.

Conclusion

The concept of smart cities holds great promise for enhancing urban life, but it also brings with it the potential for unprecedented surveillance, control, and inequality. The data delusion—the belief that more data always leads to better outcomes—must be critically examined and challenged. As we continue to build the cities of the future, we must ensure that the technologies deployed are used ethically, transparently, and with respect for the fundamental rights of all citizens. Only then can smart cities truly become spaces of opportunity, innovation, and freedom, rather than instruments of surveillance and control.

The Western Dilemma: Economic Policies and the Future of Smart Cities

The ambition to create "smart cities" is a vision many Western nations share. These cities promise efficient infrastructure, seamless connectivity, and enhanced quality of life through the integration of technology into every facet of urban living. However, this utopian vision faces significant obstacles, influenced by current economic policies, unchecked migration, the offshoring of manufacturing to China, and the aggressive push towards reducing fossil fuel dependency. Collectively, these factors threaten to undermine the West's ability to build and sustain smart cities.

Economic Policies and Fiscal Strain

Current economic policies in many Western countries are straining public finances. High levels of public debt, driven by expansive welfare states and ageing populations, limit the financial flexibility needed for the significant investments required to develop smart cities. Infrastructure projects, technological upgrades, and sustainable urban planning demand robust and consistent funding. However, with national budgets stretched thin, these investments become difficult to prioritize.

Moreover, the rising cost of living, inflation, and economic inequalities are diverting attention and resources away from long-term infrastructure projects. Policymakers are often forced to address immediate economic challenges rather than invest in future-oriented smart city initiatives. This short-term focus is detrimental to the holistic and sustained planning required to transform urban landscapes fundamentally.

Migration and Social Integration

The influx of migrants from developing nations into the West presents both opportunities and challenges. While migration can lead to cultural enrichment and economic contributions, it also places substantial pressure on urban infrastructure. Many cities are already grappling with housing shortages, congested public services, and social integration challenges. The sudden and unregulated influx of migrants exacerbates these issues, straining resources that could otherwise be allocated to smart city projects.

Moreover, the social and cultural integration of diverse populations is a complex process that demands significant investment in education, social services, and community-building efforts. These investments, while essential for societal cohesion, divert resources and focus away from the technological and infrastructural advancements necessary for smart city development.

Offshoring of Manufacturing and Economic Sovereignty

The migration of manufacturing bases to China has profound implications for Western economies. While globalization has driven down consumer costs, it has also led to the deindustrialization of many Western regions. This shift has eroded the industrial base needed for large-scale manufacturing and technological innovation within these countries.

Smart cities require a robust manufacturing sector to produce the necessary technology and infrastructure components locally. Dependence on foreign manufacturing, particularly from geopolitical rivals, poses significant risks. Supply chain disruptions, trade tensions, and intellectual property concerns can all undermine the stability and reliability of smart city developments. By offshoring manufacturing, Western nations have weakened their economic sovereignty and reduced their capacity to independently build and maintain smart city infrastructure.

Transition from Fossil Fuels and Energy Security

The push to reduce fossil fuel dependency is essential for combating climate change, but it also presents significant challenges. Transitioning to renewable energy sources requires substantial investment in new infrastructure, technology, and workforce retraining. While these efforts are crucial for long-term sustainability, they are expensive and time-consuming.

Moreover, the current renewable energy technologies are not yet fully capable of meeting the energy demands of advanced smart cities. Energy storage, grid stability, and scalability remain significant challenges. In the interim, the reduced reliance on fossil fuels could lead to energy shortages or increased energy costs, complicating the development and maintenance of energy-intensive smart city technologies.

Conclusion: A Complex Web of Challenges

The dream of building smart cities for the 21st century is increasingly at odds with the current economic and geopolitical realities facing Western nations. Economic policies focused on short-term fixes, the pressures of unregulated migration, the offshoring of manufacturing, and the complexities of transitioning to renewable energy collectively signal a challenging road ahead.

To navigate these challenges, Western nations must adopt a more strategic and long-term approach. This includes rethinking economic policies to prioritize sustainable investments, managing migration more effectively to ensure social stability, revitalizing local manufacturing capabilities, and accelerating innovations in renewable energy technologies. Only through a coordinated and comprehensive strategy can the West hope to overcome these hurdles and realize the vision of smart cities that enhance the quality of life for all their inhabitants.

So, what is your Government doing about these challenges/ Currently in Canada? Nothing that works!

The Challenge of Building Smart Cities with Limited Resources
Introduction
The concept of smart cities has captivated urban planners and policymakers worldwide. These cities, characterized by their integration of advanced technologies to enhance the quality of life, streamline services, and promote sustainability, represent a forward-thinking approach to urban development. However, the realization of smart cities is not uniform across all regions. Particularly in areas with a limited tax base, lack of wealth-creating opportunities, a deficient educational system, and significant immigration of uneducated and unskilled labour, the construction and maintenance of smart cities face substantial obstacles. This article delves into these challenges and explores potential pathways to mitigate them.
The Financial Hurdle

Building a smart city requires significant financial investment. The infrastructure needed for high-speed internet, smart grids, advanced transportation systems, and various IoT devices is capital-intensive. However, regions with a limited tax base struggle to generate the necessary revenue for these investments. A constrained tax base often results from low economic activity, which, in turn, is influenced by several factors, including poor educational systems and limited wealth-creating opportunities.

The Role of Education and Wealth Creation

A robust educational system is a cornerstone of economic development. It equips the workforce with the skills needed to engage in productive, high-value activities that drive economic growth. In regions where educational systems are underfunded or ineffective, the workforce often lacks the skills necessary for employment in advanced industries. This deficiency perpetuates a cycle of low income and limited economic development, thereby shrinking the tax base further.

Wealth creation is another critical component. Industries that generate substantial economic value, such as technology, finance, and advanced manufacturing, are typically the backbone of a thriving economy. However, regions without access to these industries, either due to geographical, infrastructural, or policy constraints, struggle to create wealth. This limitation restricts the financial resources available for public investment, including the development of smart cities.

The Impact of Immigration

Immigration can significantly influence a region's economic and social dynamics. While immigration has the potential to contribute positively to economic growth, it presents challenges when the incoming population consists largely of uneducated and unskilled labour. These individuals often find it difficult to secure well-paying jobs, thereby contributing less to the tax base. Moreover, integrating large numbers of unskilled labourers into the economy can strain public services, including education, healthcare, and housing, further diverting resources from potential smart city projects.

Bridging the Gap: Potential Solutions

While the challenges are formidable, they are not insurmountable. Several strategies can help bridge the gap and pave the way for the development of smart cities, even in resource-constrained regions.

1. Educational Reform and Investment: Prioritizing education and vocational training can equip the workforce with the skills needed for high-value jobs. Partnerships between governments, private sectors, and educational institutions can create programs tailored to local economic needs, fostering a more skilled and adaptable workforce.

2. Economic Diversification: Encouraging the development of diverse industries can reduce dependency on any single sector and create multiple avenues for wealth generation. Governments can incentivize innovation and entrepreneurship through tax breaks, grants, and supportive policies.

3. Targeted Immigration Policies: Implementing immigration policies that balance the need for labour with the skills required for economic development can help. Providing educational and vocational training for immigrants can facilitate their integration into the economy and enhance their contributions to the tax base.

4. Public-Private Partnerships (PPPs): Engaging the private sector in the development of smart city infrastructure can alleviate the financial burden on public resources. PPPs can leverage private investment and expertise, accelerating the development and deployment of smart technologies.

5. Incremental Development: Instead of attempting to transform entire cities at once, a phased approach focusing on specific sectors or regions can make the process more manageable and financially feasible. Pilot projects can demonstrate the benefits of smart technologies, garnering public and private support for broader initiatives.

6. International Aid and Cooperation: Seeking support from international organizations and more developed nations can provide the necessary funding and expertise. Collaborative projects can bring advanced technologies and best practices to regions struggling with limited resources.

Conclusion

The dream of smart cities remains an aspirational goal for many regions around the world. However, the barriers presented by a limited tax base, inadequate educational systems, and the influx of unskilled labour cannot be ignored. Addressing these fundamental issues through strategic investments, policy reforms, and innovative partnerships is essential. While the path is challenging, it is not impossible. With concerted effort and a multifaceted approach, even regions with constrained resources can move closer to the vision of smart, sustainable, and prosperous cities.

Part II: Electric Vehicles: The Promise and the Peril

The EV Revolution: Accelerating into a Brick Wall?

The past decade has witnessed a transformative shift in the automotive industry, driven by the rise of electric vehicles (EVs). Promising to reduce carbon emissions, decrease reliance on fossil fuels, and reshape the future of personal and commercial transportation, EVs have gained substantial momentum globally. Governments, automakers, and consumers have embraced this change, foreseeing a cleaner, more sustainable future. However, as the pace of EV adoption accelerates, several emerging challenges threaten to stall this revolution, creating a metaphorical "brick wall" that must be addressed for a smooth transition to a greener future.

The Rise of Electric Vehicles: A New Era in Transportation

Electric vehicles have been around for more than a century, but it is only in recent years that they have begun to gain significant traction. Technological advancements, increasing environmental awareness, and supportive government policies have fueled the surge in EV popularity. Companies like Tesla, Nissan, Chevrolet, and more recently, traditional automotive giants such as Ford, Volkswagen, and General Motors have invested billions in developing electric models, significantly expanding the range of options available to consumers.

Sales of electric vehicles have surged worldwide, with 2020 and 2021 being particularly pivotal years. According to the International Energy Agency (IEA), global EV sales more than doubled in 2021, reaching 6.6 million, representing nearly 9% of the global car market, up from 4.1% in 2020. Governments across Europe, North America, and Asia have implemented aggressive policies to promote EV adoption, including subsidies, tax incentives, and stringent emission regulations, all aiming to phase out internal combustion engines (ICEs).

The broader vision is clear: by 2030 or 2040, many countries aim to see the majority, if not all, new vehicle sales being electric. However, as the world rushes headlong into this EV revolution, several significant hurdles have begun to emerge, threatening the optimistic timelines and targets set by various stakeholders.

Emerging Challenges in the Mass Adoption of Electric Vehicles

Supply Chain Constraints and Material Shortages

One of the most pressing challenges facing the EV industry is the issue of supply chain constraints, particularly regarding critical materials like lithium, cobalt, and nickel. These materials are essential components in the lithium-ion batteries that power most electric vehicles. However, their supply is limited, and mining them presents environmental and ethical concerns. For instance, cobalt mining in the Democratic Republic of the Congo has been linked to poor labour practices and environmental degradation. As demand for EVs grows, so too does the strain on these already limited resources, potentially leading to price volatility and bottlenecks in production.

Additionally, the global semiconductor shortage that began in 2020 has affected the automotive sector, including EV manufacturing. Semiconductors are crucial for EVs, given their reliance on electronic systems and software. Delays in semiconductor supplies have led to production slowdowns, highlighting the fragility of the current EV supply chain.

Insufficient Charging Infrastructure

While the internal combustion engine vehicle has the advantage of an extensive network of fueling stations worldwide, the same cannot be said for electric vehicles. The existing charging infrastructure is insufficient to support the mass adoption of EVs. Even in countries with relatively advanced charging networks, such as Norway, the United States, and the Netherlands, the ratio of charging stations to EVs is not keeping pace with the surge in sales.

Range anxiety—the fear of running out of battery power without access to a charging station—remains a significant concern for potential EV buyers. The deployment of fast chargers, which can significantly reduce charging times, is essential but costly. Building an extensive, reliable, and fast-charging network will require massive investment, collaboration between governments and private companies, and standardized charging technologies to ensure compatibility and convenience for users.

Grid Capacity and Energy Demand

The widespread adoption of electric vehicles poses significant challenges to existing power grids. EVs require substantial energy for charging, and as their numbers increase, so does the demand on the electrical grid. In regions where the grid is already strained or where energy production is not yet fully sustainable, the additional demand from millions of EVs could lead to instability, power outages, or increased dependence on fossil fuels for energy generation, counteracting the environmental benefits of EVs.

Grid modernization is essential to accommodate the projected surge in electricity demand. This involves investing in smart grids, energy storage solutions, and the integration of renewable energy sources to ensure a stable, sustainable power supply. However, these changes are complex, expensive, and time-consuming, creating another potential obstacle to the smooth adoption of electric vehicles.

Battery Technology and Recycling Issues

While battery technology has improved dramatically, enabling longer ranges and faster charging, significant challenges remain. Current lithium-ion batteries are expensive, have a limited lifespan, and are difficult to recycle. End-of-life batteries pose a potential environmental hazard if not properly managed. Developing cost-effective, sustainable recycling methods is critical to minimizing the environmental impact of widespread EV adoption.

Furthermore, breakthroughs in battery technology, such as solid-state batteries, could revolutionize the EV market by offering greater energy density, faster charging, and improved safety. However, these technologies are still in the research and development phase and may not be commercially viable for several years. Until then, the limitations of current battery technology will continue to pose challenges to mass EV adoption.

Cost and Affordability Barriers

Despite the declining costs of EVs and the availability of government incentives, electric vehicles remain relatively expensive compared to their internal combustion engine counterparts. The high initial cost, primarily due to expensive battery packs, continues to be a barrier for many consumers, particularly in developing countries. While the total cost of ownership (TCO) for EVs can be lower due to savings on fuel and maintenance, the upfront cost can deter potential buyers.

The affordability challenge is exacerbated by inflation, rising material costs, and economic uncertainties. Without further cost reductions and innovative financing solutions, such as leasing models or battery-as-a-service, achieving mass-market appeal for EVs remains a complex challenge.

Navigating the Road Ahead: Overcoming the Brick Wall

While these challenges may seem daunting, they are not insurmountable. The future of electric vehicles will depend on the industry's ability to innovate, adapt, and overcome these obstacles. Collaborative efforts between governments, automakers, technology companies, and energy providers will be crucial in developing comprehensive solutions.

Investment in research and development for new battery technologies, sustainable mining practices, robust recycling systems, and smart grid infrastructure must continue to advance. Simultaneously, expanding charging networks, creating standardized charging solutions, and reducing the cost of EVs through economies of scale and policy support will be essential to sustain momentum.

Ultimately, the EV revolution is not just about replacing internal combustion engines with electric ones; it is about reimagining the entire ecosystem of transportation, energy, and infrastructure. The road may be fraught with challenges, but with strategic foresight, innovation, and cooperation, the world can navigate around the "brick wall" and accelerate toward a more sustainable and electrified future.

Charging Chaos: The Grid's Breaking Point

Investigating Whether Current Electrical Grid Infrastructures Can Support Widespread EV Adoption

The global push towards sustainability is reshaping the automotive industry at an unprecedented pace. Electric vehicles (EVs) have emerged as a cornerstone of this transformation, with promises of reducing carbon emissions, curbing air pollution, and weaning the world off fossil fuels. However, the rapid adoption of EVs brings with it a lesser-discussed but equally significant challenge: can our existing electrical grid infrastructures withstand the surge in demand?

The Surge in Electric Vehicles and Energy Demand

Electric vehicles, from sleek sedans to robust trucks, are becoming increasingly popular worldwide. Projections suggest that EVs could constitute up to 30% of all vehicles on the road by 2030, translating to tens of millions of electric cars, trucks, and buses drawing power from national grids. While the benefits of this shift are manifold, the question arises: Is our current electrical grid ready to handle the demand that this influx of EVs would generate?

The electricity consumption of an EV is significant. A typical electric car may require around 30 kWh to travel 100 miles. For a single vehicle, that might seem manageable. However, when scaled to millions of vehicles, the cumulative demand on the grid can be staggering. If not planned carefully, this surge in electricity demand could lead to an imbalance in the grid, causing blackouts, increased costs, and operational instability.

The Current State of Electrical Grid Infrastructures

The electrical grids that power most countries today were built in a different era, primarily designed for a one-way flow of electricity from centralized power plants to consumers. This traditional grid architecture faces several challenges when confronted with the complexities of modern energy demands, which include decentralized generation (e.g., solar, wind), two-way energy flows, and, importantly, the high energy requirements of charging EVs.

Capacity Constraints:

Many national grids already operate close to their capacity, especially during peak times. The addition of millions of EVs could overwhelm the system. For instance, a study by the International Energy Agency (IEA) indicates that widespread EV adoption could increase electricity demand by as much as 25% in certain regions. This additional burden may expose the grid's fragility, especially if charging clusters occur during peak electricity usage times, such as in the evening.

Ageing Infrastructure:

Many parts of the world's electrical grids were constructed decades ago, with ageing infrastructure that is already struggling to meet current demands. The added load of millions of EVs could exacerbate wear and tear, leading to more frequent failures and increased maintenance costs. Furthermore, these older grids often lack the digital sophistication required for advanced load management, exacerbating the risks of overloads and outages.

Geographic Disparities:

The ability of the grid to support EVs is highly dependent on location. Urban centres might be better equipped due to more substantial infrastructure investments, but rural and less populated areas could face significant challenges. Grid reliability varies greatly, meaning that certain regions may experience more frequent outages or be incapable of supporting extensive charging networks.

The Strain on Peak Demand

A key challenge with EV adoption is its impact on peak demand. EV owners are likely to charge their vehicles during the evenings when they return home from work, coinciding with peak residential electricity use for heating, cooling, and lighting. This simultaneous demand can lead to spikes in consumption that exceed grid capacity, known as "peak demand." Unless carefully managed, this could necessitate more fossil fuel-powered "peaker" plants or lead to rolling blackouts.

Potential Solutions for Grid Modernization

To prevent the "charging chaos" from overwhelming the grid, a series of infrastructural upgrades, policy shifts, and technological innovations are required:

Smart Grid Technology and Demand Response:

The transition from traditional grids to "smart grids" is crucial. Smart grids incorporate digital technology to monitor, manage, and respond to changes in electricity demand. Advanced metering infrastructure (AMI) can enable dynamic pricing, incentivizing consumers to charge their EVs during off-peak hours. Utilities can also implement demand response programs that temporarily reduce non-essential electricity consumption during peak times to balance the load.

Distributed Energy Resources (DERs):

Integration of distributed energy resources, such as solar panels, wind turbines, and energy storage systems, can provide local energy generation and alleviate grid stress. For example, solar panels combined with home battery storage can charge EVs without drawing from the grid during peak hours. This decentralized approach reduces the reliance on the grid and enhances resilience.

Investment in Grid Infrastructure:

Significant investment is required to upgrade ageing infrastructure, enhance transmission capacity, and build new substations to support high-demand areas. Reinforcing the grid with advanced control systems, flexible AC transmission systems (FACTS), and high-voltage direct current (HVDC) transmission can help manage the complex energy flows associated with large-scale EV charging.

Vehicle-to-Grid (V2G) Technology:

V2G technology allows EVs to act as mobile energy storage units that can discharge electricity back to the grid during peak demand periods. By acting as distributed energy sources, EVs can help stabilize the grid and provide ancillary services like frequency regulation.

However, widespread implementation of V2G requires significant advances in grid management technology and a conducive regulatory environment.

Policy and Regulatory Support:

Governments and regulatory bodies need to play a proactive role in facilitating grid modernization. Policies encouraging investment in renewable energy sources, smart grids, and infrastructure upgrades are crucial. Regulatory support for dynamic pricing models, demand response programs, and V2G technology can accelerate grid adaptation to meet the challenges of widespread EV adoption.

The Road Ahead: Balancing EV Adoption with Grid Stability

The shift to electric vehicles is inevitable, driven by climate policies, technological advancements, and consumer demand. However, to prevent the grid from reaching its breaking point, a comprehensive strategy is essential—one that involves collaboration between policymakers, utilities, technology providers, and consumers.

While the challenges are significant, they are not insurmountable. A forward-looking approach that combines technological innovation, strategic investments, and policy support can ensure that the benefits of EVs are not overshadowed by unintended consequences on the electrical grid. The key lies in embracing a holistic approach that not only focuses on the vehicles themselves but also on the broader energy ecosystem that will sustain them.

If we are to avoid "charging chaos," now is the time to act—to modernize our grids, innovate our technologies, and prepare our infrastructure for a future where clean energy and electric vehicles work hand in hand to create a sustainable, resilient, and reliable energy landscape.

The Additional Load on a Smart City Power Grid: The Impact of Electric Vehicles and Charging Networks

Urban centres worldwide are evolving into smart cities, leveraging advanced technologies to improve the quality of life. Electric vehicles (EVs), with their potential to reduce emissions and reliance on fossil fuels, play a critical role in this transformation. However, the rapid push for EV adoption, driven largely by government mandates, often overlooks the substantial impact on power generation and grid infrastructure. My article examines the additional load on smart city power grids from EVs and their charging networks, highlighting the challenges and potential solutions.

The Ideological Push for Electric Vehicles

Governments around the globe are aggressively promoting electric mobility as part of their environmental and sustainability agendas. These initiatives are driven more by ideological commitments to reduce carbon footprints and achieve climate goals than by pragmatic considerations of power generation and grid capacity. As a result, the increasing number of EVs on the road will place significant and sometimes unforeseen demands on urban power grids.

Increased Demand and Load Management

The integration of EVs into urban environments leads to a marked increase in electricity demand. Unlike traditional fuel stations, EV charging stations depend on the electrical grid, adding a new and substantial load which they have not planned for. The Canadian Government is forecasting 460,000 new EV charge points in the next 10 years! So, build more power stations, etc. Laughable!

This increased demand challenges power grid operators to ensure a reliable supply without compromising grid stability. Brownouts, anyone?

EV charging patterns, often concentrated during peak hours, can exacerbate this issue. For instance, many EV owners may prefer to charge their vehicles overnight at home, leading to high demand during off-peak hours. Conversely, public charging stations may see spikes in usage during the day, particularly in commercial and business districts.

The irregularity and unpredictability of these patterns require advanced load management strategies to prevent grid overloads and blackouts.

Grid Infrastructure and Capacity

Many urban power grids may not be equipped to handle the additional load of widespread EV adoption. Upgrading grid capacity involves significant investment in new substations, transformers, and distribution networks. These upgrades must be strategically planned to accommodate future growth in EV numbers and the corresponding increase in electricity consumption.

Integration of Renewable Energy

Smart cities are increasingly being coerced into integrating renewable energy sources, such as solar and wind, into their power grids. While this reduces reliance on fossil fuels, it also introduces variability in power generation. Managing the balance between supply and demand becomes more complex with the addition of EV charging loads. Effective integration of renewable energy sources requires advanced grid management systems and energy storage solutions to ensure a stable and reliable power supply.

Public vs. Private Charging Networks

Public charging stations are essential for supporting EV users who do not have access to private charging facilities. Particularly apartment dwellers. These stations are typically located in public areas such as parking lots, commercial centres, and highways. The deployment of public charging infrastructure requires careful planning to ensure adequate coverage and accessibility.

Public charging networks also need to be scalable to accommodate future growth in EV adoption. This scalability involves not only increasing the number of charging stations but also upgrading the power capacity of these stations to support faster-charging technologies. High-power chargers, which can recharge an EV battery in a matter of minutes, place significant instantaneous demand on the power grid, necessitating robust infrastructure and effective load-balancing strategies.

Private charging stations, primarily located at homes and workplaces, contribute to the overall demand on the power grid. Residential charging, in particular, presents unique challenges due to the potential for high concurrent usage during off-peak hours. Encouraging EV owners to install smart chargers that can optimize charging times based on grid demand can help mitigate these challenges.

Workplace charging stations offer an opportunity to distribute the load more evenly throughout the day. Employers can incentivize daytime charging, which aligns with solar power generation peaks, thereby reducing the strain on the grid during evening hours. Additionally, integrating workplace charging with building energy management systems can enhance load balancing and energy efficiency.

Solutions and Strategies

The deployment of smart grid technologies is crucial for managing the additional load from EVs. Smart grids use advanced sensors, communication networks, and real-time data analytics to monitor and control electricity flows. These technologies enable dynamic load management, allowing grid operators to adjust supply and demand in response to changing conditions.

But, again requires sufficient power to be generated and a grid to be built to manage said power.

Vehicle-to-Grid (V2G) Integration

Vehicle-to-Grid (V2G) technology we are informed, presents a promising solution for balancing the power grid. V2G allows EVs to not only draw power from the grid but also feed energy back into it. During peak demand periods, EVs can act as mobile energy storage units, supplying electricity to the grid and helping to stabilize it. This bidirectional energy flow requires sophisticated control systems and regulatory frameworks to ensure seamless integration.

So, pay premium rates to charge your EV and the power company will buy it back at a cheaper rate as required and leave you fully charged for your morning commute! Could not stop. Laughing at reading the various articles touting the benefits of V2G technology!

Distributed Energy Resources (DERs)

The integration of distributed energy resources (DERs), such as rooftop solar panels and home energy storage systems, can alleviate the pressure on the grid from EV charging. DERs enable localized generation and storage of electricity, reducing the reliance on centralized power plants and transmission networks. Of course, we can all afford to buy expensive solar panels and batteries from China.

Demand Response Programs

We also have demand response programs that incentivize consumers to adjust their electricity usage during peak periods. For EV charging, this can involve time-of-use pricing, where electricity rates vary based on demand. By charging their vehicles during off-peak hours, EV owners can benefit from lower rates while helping to balance the grid. Maybe easier than doing your washing and drying at 2 am?

Conclusion

EVs are costing car companies money, consumers are not exactly enthralled with buying them, and power generation and infrastructure are years away from supporting them, but the Government is pushing them...

The Impracticality of Adding 90 GW of Electricity in 12 Years for an Unwanted and Unproven Green Energy Future

As the Canadian government pushes for the widespread adoption of electric vehicles (EVs) to combat climate change, the demand for a robust charging infrastructure has skyrocketed. This ambitious mandate calls for the installation of 470,000 EV chargers, requiring an additional 90 gigawatts (GW) of electricity within 12 years. While the goal of transitioning to a greener transportation system is presented as a solution to environmental challenges, the practicalities of rapidly expanding our energy generation capabilities—especially when most of the population does not support this mandate—are daunting and questionable.

Understanding the Scale

To comprehend the challenge, consider that 90 GW of power is equivalent to constructing about 90 new large power plants, each with a capacity of 1 GW. This involves not only the construction but also navigating through regulatory, environmental, and logistical hurdles.

Nuclear Power: A Lengthy and Complex Process

Construction Time: 5-10 years

Materials Required: 500,000 - 1,000,000 cubic meters of concrete, 40,000 - 80,000 tons of steel

Land Use: 1-4 square miles per plant

Nuclear power plants are known for their high capacity and reliability. However, the average construction time for a nuclear plant ranges from 5 to 10 years, excluding the time needed for planning and regulatory approvals. The substantial materials required for these plants further complicate rapid deployment. Building enough nuclear plants to meet the additional 90 GW demand within 12 years is impractical.

Coal Power: Environmental and Regulatory Hurdles

Construction Time: 4-7 years

Materials Required: 200,000 - 400,000 cubic meters of concrete, 15,000 - 25,000 tons of steel

Land Use: 1-3 square miles per plant

Coal power plants can be built slightly faster than nuclear plants, with typical construction times of 4 to 7 years. However, environmental and regulatory barriers to building new coal plants are significant, particularly with the global emphasis on reducing carbon emissions. Extensive pollution control measures add to both time and cost, making the rapid expansion of coal power impractical.

Hydroelectric Power: Extensive Land and Time Requirements

Construction Time: 5-15 years

Materials Required: Over 1,000,000 cubic meters of concrete, tens of thousands of tons of steel

Land Use: Variable, often extensive due to reservoir creation

Hydroelectric dams can provide large amounts of power but require extensive construction periods, often between 5 to 15 years. The land requirements for these projects are substantial, as they typically involve creating large reservoirs, which can inundate significant areas. The ecological and social impacts lead to lengthy approval processes, making rapid expansion of hydroelectric power impractical.

Wind Power: Space and Material Considerations

Construction Time: 2-5 years

Materials Required: 300,000 - 400,000 cubic meters of concrete, 45,000 - 80,000 tons of steel

Land Use: 50-100 square miles for 1 GW

Wind farms can be constructed relatively quickly, with typical timeframes of 2 to 5 years. However, the space required for wind turbines is vast—often 50-100 square miles for a 1 GW capacity. While land between turbines can be used for other purposes, the sheer number of turbines needed (about 300-400 for 1 GW) presents logistical and community acceptance challenges.

Solar Power: Rapid Deployment but Large Area Needed

Construction Time: 1-3 years

Materials Required: Silicon, steel/aluminium frames, glass/plastics, cabling

Land Use: 5-10 square miles for 1 GW

Solar farms offer the quickest deployment times, generally between 1 to 3 years. However, to achieve 90 GW, a considerable amount of land is required—around 450-900 square miles. The manufacturing of solar panels also involves significant materials, and the integration of such a vast amount of solar power into the grid poses additional technical challenges.

Conclusion: The Impossibility of the Task

Given the complexities involved in constructing various types of power plants, adding 90 GW of new capacity within 12 years is highly impractical. Nuclear and hydroelectric plants take too long to build; coal plants face regulatory and environmental challenges; wind farms require vast areas and substantial materials; and while solar farms can be built quickly, they still require large tracts of land and significant materials.

Achieving such an ambitious target would require unprecedented levels of coordination, investment, and regulatory reform, alongside advances in construction technology and grid integration. While the Canadian government's goal of supporting widespread adoption of EVs with 470,000 chargers is positioned as a noble cause, albeit without supporting facts, the practical challenges and the unproven efficacy of such green energy strategies make it an unlikely and potentially misguided prospect within the proposed timeframe.

Policymakers must consider these realities and explore more feasible and proven approaches to meeting our future energy needs. Moreover, imposing such a mandate against the wishes of the majority of the population risks not only technical failure but also widespread public discontent, increased tax burden and national debt. The government must align its green energy goals with both public sentiment and practical feasibility to ensure a sustainable and supported transition to a cleaner future.

Rising Insurance Costs for Apartment Blocks with EV Charging Stations: A New Challenge for Property Owners

The growth of electric vehicles (EVs) has led to an increase in the installation of EV charging stations in apartment blocks across the country. However, this trend is accompanied by significant insurance challenges, primarily due to the elevated risk of fires associated with EV batteries. The proximity of vehicles in parking garages exacerbates this risk, potentially leading to devastating fires and extensive property damage.

EV Charging and Fire Risk

The risk of fire stems from the lithium-ion batteries that power EVs. While these batteries are generally safe, they are susceptible to a condition known as thermal runaway. This occurs when an increase in temperature leads to an uncontrollable rise in battery temperature, potentially resulting in intense fires that are difficult to extinguish and produce toxic fumes. The confined spaces of parking garages, where vehicles are parked closely together, heighten the potential for a fire to spread rapidly, causing significant damage.

Insurance Challenges

As a result, insurance companies are responding with increased premiums for apartment blocks equipped with EV charging stations. These higher premiums reflect the substantial risk of property damage and liability claims in the event of a fire. Insurers may also impose specific exclusions or conditions on policies. These could include requirements for enhanced fire detection and suppression systems, regular maintenance of charging infrastructure, and strict adherence to safety standards for EV charging equipment.

Determining liability in the event of a fire adds another layer of complexity. Liability issues can arise concerning whether the fault lies with the vehicle owner, the manufacturer of the EV or charging equipment, or the property owner. This complexity can lead to prolonged litigation and disputes over insurance coverage.

Mitigation Strategies and Insurance Requirements

To address these challenges, property owners may need to adopt several mitigation strategies. Enhanced fire safety measures, such as advanced fire detection and suppression systems tailored for lithium-ion battery fires, are essential. This could involve installing automatic sprinkler systems, fire-resistant barriers between parking spaces, and specialized firefighting equipment.

Regular inspections and maintenance of the EV charging infrastructure are also crucial. Insurers may require periodic checks on electrical systems, cable integrity, and the condition of charging units to ensure they remain in safe working order. Comprehensive risk assessments conducted in collaboration with fire safety experts and EV charging specialists can help identify potential hazards and implement measures to mitigate them, potentially leading to more favourable insurance terms.

Educating residents about the safe use of EV chargers, the importance of regular vehicle maintenance, and emergency procedures can further reduce the likelihood of incidents and demonstrate to insurers that proactive steps are being taken to manage risk.

Broader Insurance Issues for EVs

The challenges are not confined to apartment blocks. EVs present several broader insurance issues. Higher repair costs, due to the complex electronics and specialized components of EVs, result in increased premiums. Additionally, battery replacement, often necessary after an accident even if the battery appears undamaged, significantly adds to repair costs.

Emerging risks and the lack of historical data on EV performance and longevity complicate the underwriting process for insurers, making it difficult to accurately assess risks and set premiums. Public and private charging infrastructure also needs insurance against risks such as vandalism, damage, and liability for accidents that occur during charging, with insurers requiring specific safeguards and regular inspections.

Conclusion

The integration of EV charging stations in residential settings introduces significant challenges for insurers, with the primary concern being the increased risk of fires associated with lithium-ion batteries. This necessitates higher premiums, stringent safety requirements, and comprehensive risk management strategies. As the market for EVs is undergoing forced growth with many Government mandates and incentives, collaboration between property owners, residents, and insurers is essential to mitigate risks and ensure the safe and sustainable integration of a secure EV support structure.

The Challenges of Electric Vehicles: Depreciation, Charging Costs, Safety Concerns, and Public Perception

Electric vehicles (EVs) have long been promoted as a pivotal solution for reducing carbon emissions and mitigating climate change. However, despite significant technological advancements and increasing environmental awareness, EVs have not yet achieved widespread popularity. Several factors contribute to this reluctance, including rapid depreciation, high charging costs, safety concerns related to battery fires, and the general public's hesitation to embrace green ideology fully.

Rapid Depreciation

One of the primary financial concerns for potential EV buyers is the rapid depreciation of these vehicles. EVs tend to lose value faster than their internal combustion engine (ICE) counterparts due to several factors:

Technological Advancements: The swift pace of innovation in the EV sector results in newer models with significant improvements in battery life, charging speed, and range. This makes older models quickly obsolete, driving down their resale value.

Battery Degradation: Over time, the performance of EV batteries deteriorates, reducing the range and efficiency of the vehicle. Prospective buyers of used EVs are often wary of the potential cost of replacing the battery, a significant expense that further lowers the vehicle's resale value.

Incentives and Discounts: Government incentives for new EV purchases, such as tax credits and rebates, typically do not apply to used EVs. Additionally, manufacturers often offer substantial discounts on new EV models to stimulate sales, making used EVs less attractive.

High Charging Costs

The cost and infrastructure of charging EVs pose significant challenges:

Public Charging Fees: Public charging stations frequently charge higher rates than home charging. In some regions, the cost per kilowatt-hour at public chargers can be significantly higher than residential electricity rates, making regular use of public chargers expensive.

Home Charging Setup: Installing a home charging station can be costly, involving expenses for the charger itself and potential upgrades to home electrical systems. This initial investment can be a barrier for many potential EV buyers.

Time Costs: Charging an EV, especially at standard residential outlets, takes considerably longer than refuelling an ICE vehicle. Even with fast chargers, it can take 30 minutes or more to achieve a significant charge, which is inconvenient compared to the few minutes required to fill a gas tank.

Safety Concerns: Battery Fires

A notable safety concern with EVs is the risk of battery fires. Although rare, these incidents can have severe consequences:

Thermal Runaway: EV batteries can experience thermal runaway, a chain reaction that leads to overheating and potentially fires. These incidents are challenging to extinguish and can cause significant damage.

Public Perception: High-profile incidents of EV battery fires have garnered considerable media attention, contributing to public fear and scepticism about the safety of these vehicles.

Regulatory Scrutiny: The potential for battery fires has led to increased regulatory scrutiny and more stringent safety standards, which can add to the cost and complexity of producing EVs.

Reluctance to Embrace Green Ideology

Despite growing awareness of environmental issues, there is still significant resistance to fully embracing the green ideology that EVs represent:

Economic Concerns: Many consumers prioritize economic factors over environmental benefits. The higher upfront cost of EVs, along with concerns about depreciation and charging costs, often outweigh the perceived environmental advantages.

Lifestyle and Convenience: For many, the convenience and established infrastructure of ICE vehicles are hard to give up. The limited range of some EVs and the nascent state of charging infrastructure can be significant deterrents.

Scepticism About Impact: Some members of the public remain sceptical about the actual environmental impact of EVs, considering the carbon footprint of battery production and the current reliance on non-renewable energy sources for electricity generation.

Additional Practical Difficulties

Beyond depreciation, charging costs, and safety concerns, other practical issues hinder EV adoption:

Range Anxiety: Despite improvements, many EVs still have a limited range compared to ICE vehicles, causing anxiety about the vehicle's ability to complete long trips without needing frequent recharges.

Charging Infrastructure: The number of charging stations is increasing, but they are still not as ubiquitous or reliable as gas stations. This can create challenges for long-distance travel or for those living in areas with sparse charging networks.

Battery Lifespan and Recycling: Concerns about the environmental impact of battery production and disposal persist. The extraction of materials like lithium and cobalt has significant environmental and ethical implications, and the recycling of EV batteries is still developing, presenting potential long-term environmental challenges.

Vehicle Availability and Choice: While the variety of EV models is growing, the selection is still limited compared to ICE vehicles.

Consumers looking for specific features, styles, or types of vehicles (e.g., trucks, sports cars) may find fewer options among EVs.

Conclusion

While electric vehicles offer numerous benefits, including lower emissions and reduced dependence on fossil fuels, several significant barriers to widespread adoption remain. Rapid depreciation, high charging costs, safety concerns related to battery fires, and reluctance to embrace green ideology continue to deter many potential buyers. Addressing these challenges will be crucial for the EV industry to achieve greater market penetration and fulfil its promise of a more sustainable transportation future. As technology advances and infrastructure improves, these issues may gradually be mitigated, potentially leading to broader acceptance and popularity of electric vehicles.

To save boring everyone, I took numbers from the Statistics Canada website added them up, added estimated consumption for the Government proposed EV chargers and came up with the following numbers.

By 2035, the total projected electricity consumption in Canada, including the additional requirement for 460,000 Level 3 EV chargers, is approximately 1269.3 TWh per year.

This represents a significant increase from the current total electricity generation of approximately 636.2 TWh per year in 2022/3. The supporting infrastructure for the current generation has been built up over the last 100 years or so!

This substantial new increase highlights the need for considerable investment in expanding electricity generation capacity in about 10 to 12 years.

So, the question? Who is running the madhouse?

A quick thought on requirements and timelines to implement an EV power structure not including transmission lines.

The production of Level 3 EV charging stations may involve rare earth elements such as neodymium and praseodymium for permanent magnets in electric motors, as well as dysprosium for enhancing the magnets' performance. Additionally, cerium, lanthanum, and yttrium are used in various electronic components and batteries. However, the specific rare earth elements and their quantities depend on the components and technologies used in the charging station design.

At the moment my question would be where and how we obtain those materials. China? Plus, we will need the steel, copper, etc for other components. They are not exactly off the shelf!

Now let us look at the power requirements and generation. Globally, power plants typically range from a few megawatts (MW) for smaller facilities to over a gigawatt (GW) for larger, utility-scale plants. It's essential to consider the energy mix and specific power station capacities in the region of interest for a more accurate assessment.

However, the Canadian Government is asking for 460,000 charging systems over 10 years. By my calculations, that's about 90 Gigawatts.

The construction time for a 1-gigawatt (GW) power station can vary significantly based on factors such as technology, location, regulatory approvals, and project complexity. Generally, it might take several years, ranging from three to seven years or more. Factors influencing the timeline include the type of power plant (e.g., nuclear, coal, gas, or renewable energy), environmental impact assessments, permitting processes, and the availability of resources and skilled labour. Delays in any of these aspects can extend the construction timeline.

So, I will be happy to hear from engineers how wrong my figures are!

The Realities of Meeting Canadian Government Mandates for EV Charging Infrastructure

As governments worldwide, including Canada, set ambitious targets for the expansion of electric vehicle (EV) charging infrastructure, it's imperative to recognize the significant challenges and constraints that accompany these mandates. While the vision of a greener transportation future is commendable, the practicalities of material sourcing, construction timelines, and technological readiness pose formidable obstacles that cannot be overlooked.

What also cannot be overlooked is the current impracticability of EVs in the Canadian climate and the distance between cities. Other issues range from cost, repairs and rapid depreciation of EVs.

At the forefront of the discussion is the sheer scale of materials required to build and sustain the required EV charging infrastructure. From steel and copper for charging stations to rare earth metals for electronic components, the demand for these materials has skyrocketed, driven by the rapid pace of electrification. However, global supply chain disruptions, material shortages, and escalating costs have cast a shadow over the feasibility of meeting government-mandated timelines.

Furthermore, the construction and deployment of EV charging infrastructure entail intricate logistical challenges that cannot be solved overnight. Permitting processes, land acquisition, and community engagement are just a few of the hurdles that must be navigated, often resulting in delays and setbacks. The notion of rapidly scaling up EV charging infrastructure to meet government mandates within prescribed timelines may simply be unrealistic given the complexities involved.

Moreover, the transition to renewable energy sources to power EV charging infrastructure, while desirable, faces its own set of challenges. While renewable technologies such as wind and solar hold promise for reducing carbon emissions, they are not without limitations.

Intermittency, grid integration issues, and land use constraints pose significant barriers to the widespread adoption of renewable energy, particularly within the compressed timelines dictated by government mandates.

To support the planned expansion of 460,000 Level 3 EV charging stations in Canada, an estimated annual electricity consumption of approximately 1,681,920 GWh is required. Meeting this demand would necessitate substantial quantities of coal, natural gas, oil, and potentially nuclear power, given the limitations of renewable energy sources in providing consistent, on-demand power.

Coal, despite its environmental drawbacks, remains a significant part of the global energy mix. To generate the required electricity solely from coal, an estimated 2.28 billion tonnes would be needed annually. This figure represents a considerable portion of the world's known coal reserves, highlighting the immense scale of the demand. The mining of such vast quantities of coal poses significant challenges, including the environmental impact of mining operations, the health and safety risks to miners, and the logistical difficulties of transporting coal from mines to power plants. Additionally, coal-fired power plants require extensive infrastructure and maintenance, further complicating the rapid scale-up necessary to meet government mandates.

Natural gas and oil also play crucial roles in the current energy landscape. Generating the needed electricity from natural gas would necessitate large-scale extraction, processing, and transportation infrastructure. Natural gas extraction, particularly through hydraulic fracturing (fracking), raises environmental and public health concerns, including groundwater contamination and seismic activity. Similarly, oil extraction and transportation come with significant environmental risks, such as oil spills and habitat destruction. The volatility of oil and gas markets, influenced by geopolitical factors, adds another layer of complexity to ensuring a stable supply of these fuels.

Nuclear power offers a low-carbon alternative capable of providing substantial baseload power. However, the construction of nuclear power plants is an immensely complex and time-consuming process. It involves securing regulatory approvals, ensuring robust safety measures, and addressing public concerns about nuclear safety and waste disposal. The construction timelines for nuclear plants, often spanning over a decade, make them less viable for meeting short-term energy demands driven by rapid EV infrastructure expansion.

In addition to the material and logistical challenges, the rapid construction of new power plants—whether coal, gas, oil, or nuclear—faces significant regulatory and financial hurdles. Permitting processes, environmental impact assessments, and community opposition can all contribute to delays and increased costs. The financial burden of constructing new plants and upgrading existing infrastructure to support a massive increase in electricity generation also poses a formidable challenge, requiring substantial public and private investment.

While the ambition to expand EV charging infrastructure aligns with global sustainability goals, the practicalities of sourcing and utilizing the necessary materials and energy sources underscore the complexities and potential infeasibility of meeting government mandates within the proposed timelines. Addressing these challenges requires a balanced, multi-faceted approach that considers the environmental, economic, and social implications of our energy choices.

In light of these challenges, it's essential to take a pragmatic rather than ideological approach to the expansion of EV charging infrastructure. Rather than fixating solely on meeting arbitrary deadlines, policymakers should prioritize comprehensive planning, stakeholder engagement, and targeted investments in critical areas such as materials innovation and grid modernization. By adopting a long-term perspective and fostering collaboration between government, industry, communities and current or future car owners who are reluctant to purchase EVs, it might make more sense to the people who vote for them!

Pump the Brakes: Rethinking the Rush to EV Infrastructure Expansion

Fed up with the Canadian government pushing forward with plans to mandate the expansion of electric vehicle (EV) charging infrastructure, it's time to pause and reconsider whether this rush towards electrification truly reflects the desires of the public.

While the benefits of transitioning to EVs are widely touted, by the Government and its acolytes in the press – from reduced emissions to decreased reliance on fossil fuels – the reality is that many Canadians remain hesitant to embrace this change. Forcing the rapid expansion of EV infrastructure without first addressing public concerns and preferences risks alienating large segments of the population and exacerbating existing divisions.

One of the primary concerns among Canadians is the affordability and accessibility of EVs themselves. Despite advancements in technology and declining battery costs, EVs continue to carry a premium price tag compared to traditional gas-powered vehicles. For many Canadians, especially those living in rural or remote areas, condos, and apartment blocks, the prospect of investing in an EV and finding adequate charging infrastructure remains daunting.

Moreover, there is a pervasive sense of scepticism surrounding the reliability and convenience of EVs compared to their gas-powered counterparts. Concerns about range anxiety, long charging times, and the availability of charging stations persist, particularly among those who rely on their vehicles for daily commuting or long-distance travel. Until these concerns are adequately addressed, the uptake of EVs is likely to remain sluggish.

In addition to consumer hesitancy, the rush towards EV infrastructure expansion also raises questions about the allocation of resources and priorities. With pressing issues such as housing affordability, healthcare, and infrastructure maintenance competing for attention and funding, is the rapid expansion of EV infrastructure truly the most pressing concern for Canadians?

Furthermore, the environmental benefits of EVs are not as clear-cut as they may seem. While EVs produce zero tailpipe emissions, the production and disposal of EV batteries carry their environmental footprint. Without proper measures in place to ensure responsible battery recycling and disposal, the environmental gains of electrification may be offset by other factors.

Instead of forging ahead with aggressive mandates for EV infrastructure expansion, policymakers should take a step back and engage in meaningful dialogue with the public. By addressing concerns, dispelling myths, and fostering an open and transparent discussion about the future of transportation, we can ensure that any transition to EVs is truly reflective of the needs and desires of all Canadians.

In conclusion, while the push towards electrification is well-intentioned, it is essential to recognize that change cannot be forced upon the public.

Synopsis of Challenges in Implementing and Funding Canada's Energy Infrastructure Upgrade (2024-2039)

The following is a synopsis of all of the problems that will be encountered with the Business plan in my previous post due to practical considerations in implementation and funding manpower training and import and manufacturing of the required infrastructure.

1. Funding Challenges

High Capital Costs:

The total estimated cost of $850 billion to $1.7 trillion presents a significant financial challenge. Securing this level of investment requires substantial government funding, private sector involvement, and innovative financing mechanisms such as green bonds. However, obtaining consistent funding over a prolonged period (12-15 years) is challenging due to economic fluctuations and political changes.

Debt Implications:

Increasing the national debt by $70.8 billion to $141.7 billion annually could lead to a doubling of the national debt, affecting Canada's credit rating and increasing debt servicing costs. This may result in reduced public spending in other critical areas and potential public resistance to increased taxes or utility rates.

1. Private Sector Reluctance:

Private investors may be cautious due to the long payback period and high initial costs. Ensuring a favourable investment climate and risk-sharing mechanisms will be crucial to attract private capital.

2. Regulatory and Approval Hurdles

Lengthy Approval Processes:

The typical project approval process spans approximately three years, involving extensive public consultations, environmental assessments, and permitting. Delays in approvals can significantly impact project timelines and costs.

Complex Regulatory Landscape:

Navigating multiple federal and provincial regulations can be cumbersome. Coordinating between various regulatory bodies and ensuring compliance with environmental and safety standards adds complexity and potential for delays.

3. Manpower and Skills Gap

Labor Shortages:

The infrastructure upgrade will require over 200,000 skilled workers. Current shortages in skilled labour, especially in construction and renewable energy sectors, could hinder project progress. Training and upskilling programs are essential but take time to implement and yield results.

Training and Retention:

Developing comprehensive training programs to equip the workforce with the necessary skills is costly and time-consuming. Retaining skilled labour amidst a competitive job market will also be challenging, potentially leading to increased labour costs.

4. Material and Manufacturing Bottlenecks

Supply Chain Disruptions:

The large-scale demand for construction materials (steel, concrete, copper, aluminium) and renewable energy components (solar panels, wind turbines) could strain supply chains. Global supply chain disruptions, as seen during the COVID-19 pandemic, could lead to delays and increased costs.

Import Dependence:

Reliance on imported materials and components may result in vulnerabilities to geopolitical tensions, trade policies, and fluctuating import costs. Developing local manufacturing capabilities is necessary but requires significant investment and time.

5. Technological and Logistical Challenges

Technological Uncertainty:

Rapid advancements in renewable energy technologies and grid management systems mean that some components may become obsolete before the project's completion. Continuous investment in R&D and flexibility in technology adoption are required.

Logistical Complexity:

Coordinating the construction of new generation facilities, upgrading transmission lines, and deploying EV chargers across a vast geographical area like Canada is logistically complex. This involves synchronized efforts across multiple regions and sectors, which can be difficult to manage effectively.

6. Economic and Social Considerations

Public Resistance:

The financial burden on taxpayers and potential increases in utility rates could lead to public resistance. Transparent communication about the long-term benefits and economic incentives will be crucial to gaining public support.

Economic Fluctuations:

Economic downturns or shifts in global energy markets could impact funding availability and project feasibility. Flexible financial planning and robust economic policies are necessary to mitigate such risks.

Conclusion

The ambitious plan to upgrade Canada's energy infrastructure is fraught with practical challenges, including securing consistent funding, navigating regulatory hurdles, addressing manpower and material shortages, and managing technological and logistical complexities. While the long-term benefits are perhaps significant, careful planning, stakeholder engagement, and adaptive strategies are essential to overcome these challenges and ensure the successful implementation of this ideological initiative.

Business Plan Synopsis: Funding and Implementation of Canadian Energy Infrastructure Upgrade (2024-2039)

Decided to play devil's advocate on the Canadian EV mandate that's being pushed upon us. This holds for most western countries at present.

First, an outline business plan to implement their strategy, as follows.

Executive Summary

This business plan outlines a comprehensive strategy for upgrading Canada's energy infrastructure to support the projected increase in electricity demand due to economic growth, residential and industrial needs, and the deployment of 460,000 Level 3 EV chargers over the next 12-15 years. The total estimated cost ranges from $850 billion to $1.7 trillion, with annual investments between $70.8 billion and $141.7 billion. This plan addresses funding strategies, manpower and material requirements, construction timelines, regulatory considerations, and the practical challenges to ensure successful implementation.

Objectives

Increase Electricity Generation Capacity: Expand renewable energy sources and modernize existing facilities to meet the projected demand of 1269.3 TWh/year by 2035.

Enhance Transmission and Distribution Networks: Upgrade and expand the grid to support reliable and efficient energy distribution across Canada.

Deploy EV Charging Infrastructure: Install 460,000 Level 3 EV chargers along highways and in urban centres to support the widespread adoption of electric vehicles.

Promote Economic Growth and Environmental Sustainability: Foster economic development and reduce carbon emissions through sustainable energy practices.

Funding Strategies

Government Funding and Grants

Secure federal and provincial funding to support infrastructure projects.

Leverage grants and subsidies for renewable energy development.

Public-Private Partnerships (PPPs)

Collaborate with private sector partners to share costs and risks.

Attract investment from energy companies, technology firms, and financial institutions.

Green Bonds and Climate Financing

Issue green bonds to raise capital for environmentally sustainable projects.

Access international climate financing mechanisms and funds.

Tax Incentives and Rebates

Implement tax incentives for businesses and individuals investing in renewable energy and EV infrastructure.

Offer rebates for the installation of EV chargers and energy-efficient technologies.

Utility Rate Adjustments

Gradually adjust utility rates to reflect the costs of infrastructure upgrades.

Ensure rate adjustments are balanced to avoid undue financial burden on consumers.

Manpower and Material Requirements

Manpower:

Estimated requirement: Over 200,000 skilled workers across various sectors, including construction, engineering, and renewable energy technologies.

Workforce Development: Investment in training programs to upskill workers and address labour shortages.

Materials:

Construction Materials: Steel, concrete, copper, and aluminium for building generation facilities and grid infrastructure.

Renewable Energy Components: Solar panels, wind turbines, and hydroelectric equipment.

EV Chargers: High-capacity chargers, electrical components, and installation materials.

Construction Plan

Phase 1 (2024-2028): Planning and Initial Deployment

Conduct detailed feasibility studies and environmental assessments.

Begin the expansion of renewable energy sources (wind, solar, hydro).

Start upgrading high-priority transmission and distribution networks.

Install an initial batch of EV chargers in key locations.

Phase 2 (2029-2033): Major Construction and Scaling Up

Accelerate the construction of generation facilities and grid upgrades.

Scale up the deployment of EV chargers nationwide.

Implement advanced energy storage solutions to manage supply and demand.

Phase 3 (2034-2039): Completion and Optimization

Complete remaining infrastructure projects.

Optimize the grid for maximum efficiency and reliability.

Monitor and adjust strategies based on performance and emerging technologies.

Regulatory and Approval Process

Regulatory Considerations:

Compliance with federal and provincial regulations on environmental impact, safety standards, and energy efficiency.

Engage with regulatory bodies such as the Canada Energy Regulator (CER) and provincial energy boards.

Approval Requirements:

The typical project approval process spans approximately three years, including public consultations, environmental assessments, and permitting.

Continuous liaison with government agencies to expedite approvals and address regulatory challenges.

Economic Impact and Benefits

Job Creation: Generate employment opportunities in construction, engineering, and renewable energy sectors.

GDP Growth: Stimulate economic growth through large-scale investments and increased industrial productivity.

Environmental Benefits: Significantly reduce greenhouse gas emissions and enhance Canada's environmental sustainability.

Energy Security: Ensure a stable and resilient energy supply to meet future demands.

Challenges and Risk Management

Financial Risks: Secure diverse funding sources to mitigate financial risks and ensure project viability.

Technological Uncertainty: Invest in research and development to stay ahead of technological advancements.

Regulatory and Policy Hurdles: Navigate regulatory requirements and align with national and provincial policies.

Public Acceptance: Engage with communities and stakeholders to gain support and address concerns.

Conclusion

The proposed infrastructure upgrade is a strategic investment in Canada's future, addressing critical energy needs while promoting economic growth and environmental sustainability. By leveraging diverse funding sources, securing regulatory approvals, and executing a phased implementation plan, Canada can achieve its energy goals and secure a prosperous and sustainable future.

References

Canadian Taxpayers Federation

Canada Energy Regulator

Government of Canada - The Fiscal Monitor

Part III: The Battery Bottleneck: Rare Earths, Recycling, and Reality

Introduction

The global shift towards renewable energy and the electrification of transportation has sparked a surge in demand for batteries, particularly lithium-ion batteries. These batteries power everything from electric vehicles (EVs) to smartphones and laptops, making them a cornerstone of modern life. However, the production, disposal, and recycling of these batteries present significant environmental and economic challenges. The increasing demand for rare earth elements (REEs) and other critical materials such as lithium, cobalt, and nickel highlights a bottleneck in the supply chain that threatens the sustainability of battery technology. This article explores the complex interplay between rare earths, recycling, and the harsh realities of battery production and disposal.

The Demand for Rare Earth Elements and Critical Materials

Rare earth elements, despite their name, are not particularly rare but are challenging to extract in economically viable concentrations. They are crucial for a range of technologies, including batteries, magnets, and electronics. The rising demand for EVs, which require substantial quantities of lithium, cobalt, and nickel for battery production, has led to a significant increase in the extraction and processing of these materials. For instance, a single electric vehicle battery can require around 8 kg of lithium, 35 kg of nickel, and 14 kg of cobalt.

Lithium, cobalt, and nickel are at the forefront of this surge, with global reserves becoming increasingly strained. The economic and geopolitical implications of this demand are profound. More than half of the world's cobalt supply comes from the Democratic Republic of

Congo (DRC), where mining conditions are often criticized for poor labour practices and significant environmental degradation. Similarly, the extraction of lithium in regions like South America's "Lithium Triangle" (Argentina, Bolivia, Chile) raises concerns over water usage and the displacement of local communities. This intensifying demand not only drives up prices but also presents ethical and environmental challenges.

Environmental Impact of Battery Production

The extraction and processing of materials for battery production have significant environmental footprints. Lithium mining, for example, is water-intensive, requiring approximately 500,000 gallons of water per ton of lithium extracted. In arid regions such as Chile's Atacama Desert, this has led to the depletion of water resources, adversely affecting local agriculture and communities.

Cobalt mining, primarily conducted in the DRC, presents a different set of environmental and social challenges. Beyond the concerns about child labour and unsafe working conditions, cobalt extraction involves harmful processes that release toxic chemicals into the environment, contaminating water sources and soil. Nickel mining, which is mainly conducted in Indonesia, the Philippines, and Russia, also leaves behind a trail of deforestation, habitat loss, and pollution due to the release of heavy metals and sulfur dioxide.

The production process of batteries itself is energy-intensive. Manufacturing a single lithium-ion battery can emit as much as 74% more CO_2 than producing an internal combustion engine. A significant part of these emissions comes from the mining and refining of materials and the energy consumed during the battery manufacturing process, often reliant on coal or other non-renewable energy sources. As such, while EVs provide a cleaner alternative to gasoline-powered vehicles, the benefits are diminished by the carbon footprint associated with battery production.

The Recycling Challenge

Given the environmental and economic costs of extracting raw materials, recycling batteries present a potentially sustainable solution to reducing reliance on primary sources. However, battery recycling is fraught with its own set of challenges. Current recycling rates for lithium-ion batteries are surprisingly low, hovering around 5%. This is primarily due to the complexity and cost of recycling processes, which require separating and reclaiming multiple metals from each battery.

Recycling lithium-ion batteries involves several stages, including disassembly, shredding, and chemical separation. These processes are not only energy-intensive but also require significant investment in infrastructure and technology to ensure they are done safely and efficiently. Moreover, the economic viability of recycling is still limited; the cost of recovering materials often outweighs the value of the reclaimed metals, given the fluctuating prices of raw materials.

Additionally, current battery designs are not optimized for recycling. Most batteries are constructed in ways that make disassembly labour-intensive and hazardous, further increasing recycling costs. The development of "recycling-friendly" battery designs, standardized battery chemistries, and advanced recycling technologies will be crucial to overcoming these obstacles.

The Role of Policy and Innovation

Governments and industries worldwide recognize the urgency of addressing these challenges. Policy frameworks and regulations play a critical role in promoting sustainable practices in battery production and recycling. The European Union, for example, has proposed stricter regulations on battery production, mandating a certain percentage of recycled materials in new batteries and ensuring responsible sourcing of raw materials. Similar policies are being considered in the United States and China.

Innovation is also key to resolving the bottleneck in battery supply chains. Companies and researchers are exploring alternative battery chemistries that reduce or eliminate the use of rare earth elements and other critical materials. Solid-state batteries, for example, promise higher energy densities and safer performance without relying heavily on materials like cobalt. Meanwhile, breakthroughs in battery recycling technology, such as direct recycling methods and improved material recovery techniques, could dramatically improve recycling efficiency and cost-effectiveness.

The Future Outlook: A Balanced Perspective

The reality of battery production and recycling presents a stark contrast to the vision of a green, electrified future. The "battery bottleneck" is a complex web of environmental, economic, and ethical issues that must be addressed holistically. Reducing dependency on rare earths and critical materials, improving recycling rates, and fostering technological innovations are all essential components of a sustainable battery supply chain.

However, there is no single solution to this multifaceted problem. A combination of strategies, including responsible mining practices, recycling-friendly battery designs, advanced recycling technologies, and supportive policy frameworks, will be necessary to balance the demand for batteries with the environmental and economic realities of their production and disposal.

The transition to a sustainable energy future is not without its hurdles, and the journey will require cooperation among governments, industries, researchers, and consumers alike. Only by confronting these challenges head-on can we ensure that the promise of clean energy is not undermined by the unintended consequences of the battery bottleneck.

The Complex Journey of EV Lithium Batteries:

From Mines to Motors

As electric vehicles (EVs) continue to revolutionize the automotive industry, the demand for lithium-ion batteries has skyrocketed. These batteries, essential for EVs, rely on several key materials, each contributing to the battery's performance, lifespan, and safety. Here, I explore the critical materials involved, their global sources, and the intricate supply chain that brings them from mines to motors.

The Key Ingredients

Lithium

Lithium is a fundamental component of EV batteries, crucial for the cathode's energy density and overall performance. The world's leading lithium producers include Australia, Chile, Argentina, and China. Australia extracts lithium primarily from spodumene ore, while Chile and Argentina utilize brine extraction methods. Once mined, lithium is processed into lithium carbonate or lithium hydroxide, primarily in China, which dominates the refining capacity.

Cobalt

Cobalt enhances energy density and stabilizes the battery, preventing overheating and extending its lifecycle. The Democratic Republic of Congo (DRC) is the powerhouse of cobalt production, contributing over 60% of the global supply. Russia, Australia, and Canada are also significant producers. China plays a pivotal role in refining raw cobalt into battery-grade material.

Nickel

Nickel, used in the battery's cathode, boosts energy density and storage capacity. Indonesia leads global nickel production, followed by the Philippines, Russia, and Canada. The refining process, converting nickel into nickel sulfate, occurs mainly in China, Japan, and Canada.

Graphite

Graphite forms the anode due to its high electrical conductivity and stability. China is the primary producer of natural graphite, with additional sources in Brazil, India, and Canada. Both natural and synthetic graphite are processed into battery-grade anode material, predominantly in China.

Manganese

Manganese, used in some cathode chemistries, enhances stability and reduces costs. Major producers include South Africa, Australia, and Gabon. China leads in processing manganese into battery-grade manganese sulfate.

The Global Supply Chain

Mining and Extraction

Raw materials are mined globally. For example, lithium is mined from spodumene in Australia and extracted from brine in South America.

Refining and Processing

These raw materials undergo refining to become battery-grade chemicals, a process heavily centred in China. Countries like Chile, Argentina, and Australia also contribute to lithium processing.

Cathode and Anode Manufacturing

Refined materials are transformed into cathode and anode components, primarily in China, South Korea, and Japan.

Battery Cell Manufacturing

The cathodes and anodes are assembled into battery cells by major manufacturers such as CATL, LG Chem, Panasonic, and Samsung SDI, with production facilities in China, South Korea, Japan, and increasingly in Europe and the United States.

Battery Pack Assembly

Battery cells are integrated into packs, typically near automotive manufacturing hubs in the US, Germany, and China, streamlining the supply chain.

Challenges and Future Developments

Supply Chain Vulnerabilities

The concentration of processing facilities in specific countries, particularly China, poses risks. Geopolitical tensions and trade policies can impact material availability and pricing.

Environmental and Ethical Concerns

Mining activities, especially in the DRC, raise environmental and ethical issues, including child labour and poor working conditions. Efforts to improve traceability and sustainability in the supply chain are ongoing.

Technological Advancements

The research aims to develop new battery chemistries that reduce dependence on critical materials like cobalt while enhancing overall performance and safety.

In conclusion, the production of EV lithium-ion batteries is a complex, global endeavour. The journey from raw material extraction to finished battery packs involves numerous steps and locations, underscoring the intricate nature of the supply chain powering the electric vehicle revolution. This, allied with the fact that they are not popular, or will have the necessary infrastructure to support them soon, makes one wonder why they are being forced upon us.

Plugged In but Nowhere to Go: Infrastructure Gaps and Consumer Concerns

As the global push toward sustainability accelerates, electric vehicles (EVs) are becoming increasingly central to plans for reducing greenhouse gas emissions and curbing our dependence on fossil fuels. Governments, automakers, and environmentalists all seem to agree: that the future is electric. However, while sales of EVs are on the rise, a host of practical issues and infrastructure gaps are becoming evident, raising concerns among consumers and potentially stalling the green transition. This article delves into the significant infrastructure challenges faced by consumers in the adoption of electric vehicles and explores the broader implications for society.

The Surge in Electric Vehicle Adoption

Electric vehicles have experienced substantial growth in the last decade. According to the International Energy Agency (IEA), there were over 10 million electric cars on the road globally in 2020, and this number has continued to grow rapidly. Countries like Norway, China, and the Netherlands are leading the charge, offering incentives such as tax breaks, subsidies, and dedicated lanes for EVs. Consumers are increasingly drawn to electric vehicles due to their lower operating costs, government incentives, and the growing awareness of climate change. However, despite the enthusiasm and the market growth, a transition to EVs involves more than just the cars themselves. The supporting infrastructure must keep pace, or the surge in EV adoption may face significant roadblocks.

Charging Infrastructure: The Achilles' Heel

A critical factor for the widespread adoption of EVs is the availability of reliable and accessible charging infrastructure. For many consumers, "range anxiety" — the fear of running out of battery power without a nearby charging station — remains a significant deterrent. Unlike gasoline vehicles, which benefit from a dense network of fueling stations, EV charging infrastructure is still in its nascent stage in many parts of the world.

While some urban areas in Europe, North America, and parts of Asia have made strides in expanding charging networks, rural areas and developing countries lag considerably. Even in cities with relatively high EV adoption rates, charging stations can be sparse or inconveniently located. Home charging is an option for many, but not all consumers have access to a personal garage or driveway where they can install a charger. This is especially true in densely populated cities where apartment living is common. For such consumers, reliable public charging is not just a convenience—it's a necessity.

Furthermore, there are often inconsistencies in charging speeds and types. While some stations offer fast charging that can replenish a battery to 80% capacity in 30 minutes, others may take several hours to do the same. This variability can create logistical challenges, especially on long trips or in situations where a quick recharge is needed.

The Incompatibility Conundrum

Another significant concern for consumers is the issue of compatibility among charging stations. Unlike the standardized fuel nozzles of gasoline stations, EV charging ports and payment systems are not universally compatible. Different automakers often use different charging standards and connectors, creating confusion and inconvenience for users. While efforts are underway to standardize these systems, a lack of harmonization can deter potential buyers worried about accessibility and ease of use.

Moreover, there is the issue of payment systems. Some charging stations require proprietary apps, memberships, or cards, further complicating the user experience. A fragmented system where each charging provider operates in isolation only serves to increase consumer frustration and may undermine the push toward electrification.

The Cost Factor: Who Foots the Bill?

Building a comprehensive, accessible, and reliable charging infrastructure is a costly endeavour. Governments, utility companies, automakers, and private investors all play a role in this ecosystem, but the question of who should bear the brunt of the cost remains contentious. The financial burden of installing and maintaining charging stations is high, and without sufficient incentives or a clear economic model, the growth of charging infrastructure could stall.

For consumers, the cost factor is also a direct concern. While electricity is generally cheaper than gasoline, the price of charging at a public station can vary significantly. High costs at public charging stations, coupled with subscription fees or pay-per-use models, may erode some of the cost-saving benefits that make EVs attractive in the first place. For the EV revolution to succeed, the cost of charging must be competitive, transparent, and fair.

Power Grid Readiness: A Looming Challenge

As EV adoption grows, the impact on national power grids is becoming a critical concern. In regions with ageing or underdeveloped infrastructure, the sudden surge in demand for electricity could lead to blackouts or necessitate costly upgrades. Peak demand periods, such as early evenings when people return from work and plug in their vehicles, could exacerbate these issues.

To mitigate these risks, investments in smart grid technologies, energy storage systems, and renewable energy sources are essential. However, these are long-term solutions that require substantial capital investment and strategic planning. In the interim, the question of grid stability and the potential for brownouts or grid failures remains a significant concern for both consumers and policymakers.

Consumer Awareness and Education: Bridging the Knowledge Gap

Another dimension of the infrastructure challenge is the level of consumer awareness and education about electric vehicles. For many potential buyers, the complexity of charging options, the cost implications, and the differences between types of EVs (battery electric vehicles vs. plug-in hybrids) can be overwhelming. A lack of reliable information can lead to misconceptions and hesitancy.

Education campaigns, transparent information from manufacturers, and government-led initiatives can play a pivotal role in addressing these gaps. Empowering consumers with knowledge will not only alleviate some of their concerns but also help in making more informed choices.

Looking Ahead: The Road to a Seamless EV Transition

While the transition to electric vehicles is an essential component of achieving a more sustainable future, it is clear that there are still numerous challenges to overcome. Addressing the infrastructure gaps requires a coordinated effort among various stakeholders, including governments, automakers, utility providers, and consumers.

Policy interventions, such as incentivizing private investments in charging networks, setting standards for interoperability, and integrating renewable energy sources into the grid, will be critical. Moreover, fostering a culture of collaboration rather than competition among stakeholders can create a more cohesive ecosystem that benefits everyone.

The transition to electric vehicles is not merely about replacing gasoline cars with battery-powered ones. It is about reimagining the entire automotive and energy landscape. As we stand on the brink of this transformative shift, the need for a robust, reliable, and consumer-friendly infrastructure becomes increasingly evident. Without addressing these gaps, we may find ourselves "plugged in but nowhere to go."

For a sustainable and practical EV future, the journey must be as seamless as the destination.

The Impracticality of the UK's Zero Emission Vehicle (ZEV) Mandate: Ideology Over Pragmatism

The United Kingdom's ambitious Zero Emission Vehicle (ZEV) mandate, which requires car manufacturers to produce a certain percentage of zero-emission cars and vans each year up to 2030, illustrates how ideology can often outweigh practicality in policymaking. According to the mandate, by 2030, 80% of new cars and 70% of new vans sold in Great Britain must be zero-emission vehicles (ZEVs), increasing to 100% by 2035. While the government's aim to combat climate change and reduce greenhouse gas emissions is commendable, the policy overlooks significant concerns about market demand, infrastructure preparedness, and the potential economic ramifications of a rapid transition to electric vehicles (EVs). Furthermore, the policy risks allowing low-cost Chinese-made EVs to dominate the market, raising additional concerns about quality, safety, and the strategic implications of such dependence.

Consumer Reluctance Toward Electric Vehicles

One of the central flaws in the ZEV mandate is its failure to address the lack of consumer demand for electric vehicles. Despite substantial government subsidies, tax incentives, and sustained advocacy from environmental groups, many British consumers remain reluctant to switch to EVs. This hesitance stems from various factors, including the higher upfront cost of electric vehicles compared to internal combustion engine (ICE) cars, concerns about battery longevity and replacement costs, and the perceived reliability and convenience of traditional petrol and diesel vehicles.

A survey by Deloitte found that nearly half of prospective car buyers are unwilling to pay more for an electric vehicle than they would for a conventional car, even after accounting for potential savings on fuel and maintenance. Additionally, many drivers have concerns about the performance of EVs in colder climates, where battery efficiency can be significantly reduced, posing a risk of breakdowns or reduced range in adverse weather conditions.

Inadequate Charging Infrastructure

A major barrier to the widespread adoption of electric vehicles is the inadequacy of the UK's current charging infrastructure. At present, there are approximately 42,000 public charging points across the UK. To meet the government's target of 100% zero-emission vehicle sales by 2035, experts estimate that the UK would need at least 300,000 charging points by 2030—a more than sevenfold increase in less than a decade.

Achieving this is not merely a matter of scaling up numbers. The existing network is unevenly distributed, with most charging points located in urban centres and more affluent areas, while rural and less economically developed regions remain severely underserved. Without a robust and evenly distributed charging network, the mandate could deepen social inequalities, limiting access to clean transportation options for those outside major metropolitan areas.

Furthermore, the development of charging infrastructure faces significant logistical challenges. These include the need for substantial upgrades to the electricity grid, securing land and space for charging stations and navigating regulatory hurdles. The National Grid has already warned that the current infrastructure is not prepared to handle the sharp increase in demand that would accompany a mass shift to electric vehicles. Without considerable investment and planning, the rapid expansion required under the mandate is highly unlikely to materialize.

Economic Burden and Ideological Overreach

The ZEV mandate seems to be driven more by ideological commitments to environmental goals than by a grounded assessment of the practical challenges involved in transitioning to a fully zero-emission vehicle market. The economic burden of this rapid shift could be severe. The automotive industry, still reeling from the effects of Brexit, the COVID-19 pandemic, and a global semiconductor shortage, faces significant pressure to meet the stringent production targets set by the mandate. Failure to do so could result in job losses, further economic strain, and potential long-term damage to a vital UK industry.

The mandate also imposes potential costs on consumers and taxpayers, who would bear the financial burden of upgrading the national grid, installing charging infrastructure, and subsidizing the transition to electric vehicles. Such heavy-handed government intervention could stifle innovation, limiting manufacturers' ability to invest in developing better and more affordable EVs that could naturally drive consumer demand.

The Influx of Low-Cost Chinese EVs: A Strategic and Economic Risk

An often-overlooked consequence of the ZEV mandate is the potential for China to flood the UK market with low-cost electric vehicles, a prospect that raises serious concerns about economic dependency, quality, and strategic vulnerabilities. China has rapidly scaled up its EV production capabilities and already dominates global supply chains for EV batteries and components. The relatively low production costs and aggressive pricing of Chinese-made EVs could allow them to capture a significant share of the UK market, particularly as British consumers look for affordable options amid economic uncertainty.

However, many reports have raised concerns about the quality and safety standards of Chinese-manufactured vehicles, suggesting that a reliance on these imports could lead to negative outcomes for UK consumers. The "Made in China" label has been associated with lower-quality products in various sectors and allowing the UK market to be dominated by such imports could add another darker chapter to that perception. Moreover, increasing dependence on Chinese EVs could undermine the UK's domestic automotive industry, weaken its economic sovereignty, and expose it to geopolitical risks, particularly given the tense relationship between China and Western democracies.

Conclusion: A Need for Pragmatic Policy Reform

The UK's Zero Emission Vehicle mandate, in its current form, represents a well-meaning but deeply flawed approach to achieving environmental sustainability. It sets unrealistic targets without adequately addressing the underlying issues of consumer reluctance, inadequate infrastructure, economic feasibility, and the risks associated with an influx of low-cost Chinese EVs. While the goal of reducing emissions is important, it must be pursued through pragmatic, market-based strategies that consider the complexities of economic, social, and geopolitical realities.

A more sensible approach would involve setting more realistic timelines, significantly investing in infrastructure development before enforcing sales quotas, and fostering an environment where consumer choice, technological innovation, and domestic industry competitiveness can naturally drive the shift towards zero-emission vehicles. Without such reforms, the ZEV mandate risks becoming another example of poorly conceived government policy that creates more problems than it solves, both economically and strategically.

My Two Cents.

When it comes to the issue of battery degradation and the impact of repeated cold cycles on electric vehicles, I have to say that I remain sceptical about the practicality of EVs, especially in cold climates. While there's a lot of talk about the benefits of electric vehicles, I believe there are fundamental problems—like battery degradation in cold weather—that make them far less reliable and appealing than traditional internal combustion engine (ICE) vehicles.

In my opinion, one of the biggest drawbacks of EVs is how their batteries perform in cold temperatures. Unlike internal combustion engines that can function relatively well regardless of the weather, lithium-ion batteries in EVs struggle as the temperature drops. Cold weather significantly reduces battery efficiency and range, leading to a frustrating experience for drivers who have to deal with these unpredictable limitations. For those of us living in areas where winter is long and harsh, this is a serious drawback.

But what concerns me even more is how repeated exposure to freezing temperatures doesn't just cause temporary dips in performance—it accelerates the long-term degradation of the battery. Over time, these cold cycles cause irreversible damage, reducing the battery's capacity and reliability. This means that as the EV ages, its range decreases even more, making it a less practical choice for anyone who needs a dependable vehicle for daily use, especially in remote or rural areas.

Then there's the cost factor. Batteries are the most expensive part of an electric vehicle, and if they degrade faster in cold climates, that's a financial burden on the owner. I don't see why we should be pushing people to invest in EVs when they could end up facing significant replacement costs in just a few years. In contrast, internal combustion vehicles don't have this problem; they've been tried and tested in all sorts of environments and have proven to be more durable and cost-effective over the long run.

To me, this is a clear indication that we're not ready to make the switch to EVs on a large scale, especially in places that experience harsh winters. Until battery technology significantly improves to withstand cold without degrading, I see little reason to abandon the reliability of internal combustion vehicles. EVs might be fine for mild climates or short commutes, but for those who need a vehicle they can rely on in all conditions, ICE vehicles are still the superior choice.

In conclusion, while EVs are being promoted as the future of transportation, I remain unconvinced. The reality of battery degradation in cold climates is just one of many reasons I continue to prefer the tried-and-true technology of internal combustion engines. They provide the reliability, range, and cost-effectiveness that EVs, at least for now, simply can't match.

Part IV: Government Mandates and Market Realities

Mandates Without a Plan: The Problem with Top-Down Policies

In recent years, governments worldwide have been increasingly focused on policies that address environmental sustainability, technological advancement, and urban development. Among the most prominent examples are mandates for smart cities and the rapid adoption of electric vehicles (EVs). While these initiatives are undoubtedly aimed at creating a more sustainable and technologically advanced future, they often reflect a top-down approach that lacks comprehensive planning and consideration for the complexities on the ground. The problem with these mandates lies not in their objectives but in their implementation—often characterized by a lack of feasibility, infrastructure readiness, and public engagement.

The Push for Smart Cities: An Ambitious Yet Overbearing Vision

The concept of smart cities is compelling: urban areas are integrated with information and communication technology (ICT) to manage resources efficiently, reduce waste, and enhance the quality of life for citizens. The idea is to use sensors, data analytics, and IoT (Internet of Things) devices to optimize everything from traffic management to energy use. However, when governments impose smart city mandates from a central authority without sufficient groundwork, the results can be chaotic and counterproductive.

Lack of Local Context and Customization

One of the major pitfalls of top-down smart city mandates is the lack of consideration for local contexts. Cities are not homogenous entities;

they differ vastly in their geography, socio-economic conditions, existing infrastructure, and technological maturity. A smart city solution that works in a metropolitan hub like Singapore may not be viable in a mid-sized city in India or a historic town in Europe. Yet, central governments often issue blanket mandates without offering flexibility for customization. This approach forces cities to adopt a one-size-fits-all model, leading to inefficient use of resources and technologies that may not be the best fit for the local context.

Infrastructure and Resource Constraints

Building smart cities requires robust digital infrastructure, including high-speed internet connectivity, advanced data centres, and a reliable energy supply. Many cities, especially in developing countries, struggle with even basic infrastructure needs such as water supply, sewage systems, and road networks. Expecting such cities to leapfrog into smart city status without first addressing these foundational issues is unrealistic. Moreover, the high cost of deploying smart technologies can strain municipal budgets, especially when such mandates are enforced without financial support or strategic guidance from central authorities.

The Rush for Electric Vehicles: The Perils of Pushing Too Fast

Governments across the globe have aggressively promoted the adoption of electric vehicles (EVs) to combat climate change, reduce air pollution, and decrease reliance on fossil fuels. While the vision is commendable, the execution of such mandates is often fraught with challenges.

Insufficient Charging Infrastructure

One of the most significant barriers to widespread EV adoption is the lack of charging infrastructure. Many countries, particularly those that are still developing their public infrastructure, lack the widespread network of charging stations necessary to support an all-electric fleet. Top-down mandates often set aggressive deadlines for phasing out internal combustion engines without corresponding investments in charging stations, grid upgrades, or battery recycling facilities. This gap creates a scenario where consumers are forced into adopting EVs without the necessary infrastructure to support them, resulting in frustration and, in some cases, a backlash against the policies themselves.

Economic and Social Implications

The economic implications of a forced transition to electric vehicles are also significant. Mandates often fail to consider the existing automotive ecosystem, including the millions of jobs tied to the production, maintenance, and operation of traditional vehicles. A hasty shift to EVs can lead to substantial job losses, especially in countries where the automotive sector forms a large part of the economy. Furthermore, the cost of EVs is still relatively high compared to traditional vehicles, making them less accessible to middle- and lower-income households. Without subsidies, tax incentives, or affordable financing options, the mandate for widespread EV adoption risks creating a socio-economic divide.

The Need for a Bottom-Up Approach

The problems with top-down mandates for smart cities and EVs point to a broader issue with centralized policy-making: a lack of ground-level engagement, planning, and execution. A bottom-up approach is often more effective, where local governments, businesses, and communities are involved in planning and decision-making from the outset. This model encourages policies that are tailored to the specific needs, capacities, and contexts of different cities and regions.

Collaborative Planning and Incremental Implementation

Collaborative planning allows for incremental implementation, where smaller pilot projects can be tested, evaluated, and scaled up based on their success and adaptability. This approach reduces the risk of failure and enables continuous learning and adjustment. For instance, rather than mandating an entire city to transition to smart technologies, governments could start with specific sectors—like transportation or waste management—gradually expanding based on data-driven results.

Incentivizing Innovation and Flexibility

Another advantage of a bottom-up approach is that it incentivizes innovation and flexibility. By giving local authorities more control and providing financial and technical support, governments can foster an environment where innovative solutions can emerge organically. This way, policies are not only more sustainable but also more inclusive and equitable, addressing the diverse needs of different communities.

Conclusion: Rethinking the Mandate Mentality

While the urgency of transitioning to smart cities and electric vehicles is undeniable in the face of climate change and rapid urbanization, the path to achieving these goals must be reconsidered. Top-down mandates that lack thorough planning, local engagement, and infrastructure support are unlikely to succeed. Instead, a more nuanced approach that combines national vision with local empowerment, phased implementation, and continuous feedback can create a more sustainable, equitable, and successful transition to the future. The problem is not the mandates themselves but the absence of a comprehensive plan that addresses the realities on the ground.

Carrots, Sticks, and Unintended Consequences: Incentivizing Change in Urban Development and Electric Vehicle Uptake

Urban development and the shift towards sustainable transportation are complex issues that involve multiple stakeholders, policies, and economic incentives. Governments worldwide use a mix of "carrots" (subsidies and tax breaks) and "sticks" (penalties and regulations) to influence behaviour and drive societal change. However, these strategies often come with unintended consequences. This article explores the impact of such incentives on urban development and electric vehicle (EV) uptake, highlighting the delicate balance between encouraging change and avoiding unforeseen negative outcomes.

The Role of Incentives in Urban Development

Urban development policies often aim to create sustainable, livable, and economically viable cities. Governments typically use financial incentives to guide development in specific directions. For instance, subsidies may be offered to developers to encourage the construction of affordable housing or green buildings that meet certain environmental standards. Tax breaks can be provided to businesses that set up operations in underdeveloped areas, to stimulate local economies and reduce urban inequality.

These incentives can be highly effective. For example, subsidies and tax breaks have encouraged the proliferation of eco-friendly buildings, green roofs, and energy-efficient designs in cities worldwide. However, they can also lead to unintended consequences. One such example is the phenomenon of "green gentrification," where incentives for green development inadvertently increase property values, displacing low-income residents. While the policy may achieve its environmental goals, it may simultaneously undermine social equity objectives.

Moreover, subsidies can distort market dynamics. A heavy reliance on government incentives might discourage developers from investing in innovative or sustainable projects without subsidies, leading to an over-dependence on government support. This scenario could stifle the development of a truly competitive market for sustainable urban development.

Electric Vehicle Uptake: Incentives and Market Dynamics

Electric vehicles (EVs) are central to reducing greenhouse gas emissions and combatting climate change. To encourage EV adoption, governments employ a combination of financial incentives and regulatory mandates. These can range from direct subsidies for EV buyers to tax breaks for manufacturers and investments in charging infrastructure. Penalties, such as higher taxes on internal combustion engine (ICE) vehicles and congestion charges in urban areas, act as deterrents to the continued use of fossil fuel-powered cars.

On the positive side, these "carrots and sticks" have significantly boosted EV adoption rates. In countries like Norway and the Netherlands, generous incentives have led to EVs accounting for a large share of new car sales. However, the strategy is not without pitfalls. In some markets, generous subsidies have led to a surge in demand that the supply chain cannot meet, causing shortages and delays. Moreover, in regions where subsidies are abruptly reduced or removed, the EV market has sometimes experienced a sharp decline, indicating that the market is not yet self-sustaining.

Additionally, subsidies can lead to the problem of "free riders"—individuals who would have purchased an EV even without government incentives, effectively wasting public funds. This phenomenon raises concerns about the efficient allocation of resources, as the cost per ton of CO2 saved through EV subsidies can be high compared to other decarbonization measures.

Unintended Consequences and the Rebound Effect

One of the most critical issues with incentives is the unintended consequences that can arise from well-intentioned policies. For instance, subsidies for urban development may encourage developers to build in areas prone to natural disasters or environmental degradation, leading to long-term social and economic costs. Similarly, tax incentives for businesses in urban centres might inadvertently increase congestion and pollution if not paired with robust public transport and infrastructure planning.

In the case of EVs, the "rebound effect" is a notable example. This effect occurs when improvements in energy efficiency lead to increased energy consumption rather than a decrease. For instance, cheaper running costs for EVs may encourage more driving, thereby reducing the net environmental benefits. Additionally, as the number of EVs increases, so does the electricity demand. If this increased demand is met with non-renewable energy sources, the overall environmental benefits could be diminished.

Balancing Incentives for Sustainable Change

For incentives to be effective and minimize unintended consequences, a balanced and well-coordinated approach is necessary. Policymakers must design incentives that are targeted, time-bound, and capable of adapting to changing circumstances. For instance, phasing out subsidies gradually can help markets adjust and prevent sudden shocks that could undermine progress. Additionally, incentives should be linked to performance metrics, such as reducing emissions or increasing energy efficiency, to ensure that they achieve their intended outcomes.

Another approach is to combine financial incentives with non-monetary measures. For example, in urban development, zoning regulations, land use planning, and community engagement can complement subsidies and tax breaks, creating a more holistic and sustainable urban environment. For EV uptake, investing in public charging infrastructure and mandating stricter emissions standards for conventional vehicles can reinforce the impact of financial incentives.

Finally, it is crucial to conduct regular assessments of the effectiveness of these policies and be prepared to revise or withdraw incentives that are not delivering the desired outcomes or are causing negative side effects. A more nuanced approach to incentivization, which considers the complexity of urban development and sustainable transportation, can help avoid the pitfalls of one-size-fits-all policies.

Conclusion

Incentives are powerful tools for driving change, but they come with risks. While subsidies, tax breaks, and penalties can significantly influence urban development and EV uptake, they must be carefully designed and implemented to avoid unintended consequences. A balanced approach that combines financial incentives with robust planning, regulation, and stakeholder engagement can help create sustainable, equitable, and thriving urban environments and accelerate the transition to electric mobility. The challenge for policymakers is to navigate the fine line between encouraging positive change and mitigating the risks that come with it.

Innovation or Regulation: What Drives Progress?

The debate between innovation and regulation in driving sustainable change has long been a topic of discussion among policymakers, business leaders, and scholars. Both are crucial components in shaping societal progress, but they operate in fundamentally different ways. Innovation often leads to groundbreaking solutions and economic growth, while regulation provides a framework to ensure that such growth is sustainable, equitable, and safe. Understanding the interplay between these forces is essential to crafting policies that promote balanced and long-term progress.

The Power of Innovation

Innovation is often hailed as the primary engine of progress. From the invention of the steam engine to the rise of the internet and digital technologies, innovation has historically been a catalyst for economic growth and societal transformation. It allows for the creation of new markets, improves productivity, and solves complex problems by pushing the boundaries of what is possible.

Consider the technology sector as a prime example. Companies like Apple, Google, and Tesla have revolutionized industries through continuous innovation, offering new products and services that improve the quality of life, reduce inefficiencies, and open up new economic opportunities. These innovations have enabled new forms of communication, transportation, and energy production, each contributing significantly to societal progress.

Moreover, innovation drives competition, which in turn fosters further innovation. Companies constantly seek to outdo each other, leading to better products, services, and technologies. This competitive cycle generates economic value, creates jobs, and ultimately benefits consumers. In the realm of sustainable change, innovations in renewable energy, electric vehicles, and green technologies are paving the way for a more sustainable future, demonstrating that innovation can be a powerful driver of progress.

The Role of Regulation

However, unregulated innovation can have significant downsides. Rapid technological advances without appropriate oversight can lead to economic inequality, environmental degradation, and social harm. The role of regulation is to provide a structured environment in which innovation can thrive without compromising public safety, environmental sustainability, or social equity.

Regulations set standards for safety, environmental impact, and ethical practices. For example, emissions standards set by governments have pushed car manufacturers to innovate in ways that reduce pollution and greenhouse gas emissions. The regulations act as a catalyst for innovation rather than a barrier, encouraging companies to develop cleaner, more efficient technologies. This demonstrates that regulation, when well-designed, can drive innovation toward socially desirable outcomes.

Furthermore, regulations can help level the playing field. In industries where larger players could potentially dominate the market, regulations prevent monopolistic practices and promote fair competition, ensuring that smaller innovators also have the opportunity to thrive.

Regulation also protects consumers and the public interest. In areas such as pharmaceuticals, data privacy, and financial services, stringent regulations ensure that companies do not exploit consumers or engage in practices that could lead to systemic risks. For instance, the General Data Protection Regulation (GDPR) in Europe has set a global standard for data privacy, forcing companies to innovate around privacy-preserving technologies and transparent data practices.

Striking the Right Balance

The debate between innovation and regulation is not a zero-sum game; rather, it is about finding the right balance. Innovation and regulation can, and often do, complement each other. For instance, regulations can create markets for innovation. Carbon pricing and renewable energy mandates have spurred investment in clean technologies, driving down costs and scaling up adoption. Similarly, regulations that mandate fuel efficiency have led to significant innovations in automotive technology.

One of the key challenges is ensuring that regulations are adaptive and forward-looking. Rigid and outdated regulations can stifle innovation by imposing unnecessary burdens or failing to account for technological advancements. Regulatory frameworks should be designed to evolve alongside innovation, providing the flexibility needed to accommodate new technologies and business models.

Moreover, it is crucial to involve all stakeholders in the regulatory process—governments, businesses, academia, and civil society—to ensure that regulations are well-informed, balanced, and aligned with societal goals. Public-private partnerships can play a significant role in this regard, fostering a collaborative environment where innovation can be channelled toward sustainable development.

The Future of Progress: A Synergistic Approach

As we move further into the 21st century, the need for sustainable progress is more urgent than ever. Challenges such as climate change, economic inequality, and public health crises demand both innovative solutions and robust regulatory frameworks. Neither innovation nor regulation alone can drive the progress needed to address these complex issues. Instead, a synergistic approach that leverages the strengths of both is essential.

Innovators must be encouraged to push boundaries, but within a regulatory framework that ensures these advancements contribute positively to society. Conversely, regulators must remain agile, ready to update rules to accommodate and encourage beneficial innovations while mitigating potential harms.

In conclusion, progress in the modern world is not driven solely by innovation or regulation but by the dynamic interaction between the two. When properly aligned, innovation and regulation can work hand-in-hand to drive sustainable change, fostering a future that is not only technologically advanced but also equitable, inclusive, and environmentally sound. The debate, therefore, should not be about choosing one over the other, but rather about finding the most effective way to integrate both for the common good.

The Push for Electric Vehicles (EVs): Who Really Benefits?

Governments around the world have positioned electric vehicles as a central pillar of their environmental agenda. Subsidies, tax breaks, and mandates encourage consumers and automakers to switch to EVs, aiming to reduce carbon emissions and lead the charge towards a greener future. While there are undeniable benefits—such as decreased pollution and fostering innovation in green technology—these policies are not without flaws.

Pros:

- **Environmental Impact:** EVs produce fewer greenhouse gas emissions compared to traditional vehicles, especially when powered by renewable energy.
- **Technological Innovation:** The shift to EVs has spurred technological advancements, from battery development to autonomous driving capabilities, potentially leading to new industries and jobs.

Cons:

- **Consumer Costs:** The higher upfront cost of EVs compared to conventional cars is a barrier for many consumers, especially those in lower-income brackets. Subsidies help, but they are not always sufficient.
- **Taxpayer Burden:** The incentives for EVs and the development of charging infrastructure are funded by taxpayers. These costs are borne collectively, but the benefits are disproportionately enjoyed by wealthier citizens who can afford EVs.
- **Environmental and Social Costs Abroad:** The mining of lithium, cobalt, and other materials required for EV batteries often occurs in developing countries, leading to environmental degradation, poor labour conditions, and local conflicts.

In essence, while governments promote EVs as a green solution, they often overlook the inequities in how these policies affect citizens. Should we be using public funds to subsidize vehicles that remain out of reach for many? Could these resources be better spent on improving public transportation or incentivizing broader environmental initiatives that provide more inclusive benefits?

The Pushback: Citizen Reactions to Smart Cities and EV Policies

As urban landscapes worldwide undergo transformative changes driven by technology and sustainability goals, the concepts of "smart cities" and electric vehicles (EVs) have emerged as cornerstones of future urban planning. While these initiatives promise efficiency, sustainability, and improved quality of life, they have also sparked significant debate and resistance among different communities. This pushback reflects a complex interplay of economic, social, cultural, and environmental concerns. The diverse reactions from various segments of society highlight that the path to a "smart" and sustainable future is neither straightforward nor universally embraced.

1. Economic Concerns: Affordability and Accessibility

One of the primary points of resistance to smart cities and EV policies is rooted in economic concerns. Proponents of these policies often emphasize long-term savings, reduced energy consumption, and lower emissions. However, for many citizens, the initial costs associated with smart technologies and electric vehicles remain prohibitively high.

Smart Cities: Urban centres are increasingly adopting smart infrastructure, such as intelligent traffic management systems, smart grids, and IoT-enabled public services. While these innovations can lead to better resource management and improved public services, they often come with hefty price tags. Communities, especially those in low-income areas, question whether the benefits of such technologies will be equitably distributed or whether they will disproportionately benefit wealthier neighbourhoods that can afford to adopt and maintain these advancements. There is a fear that smart city initiatives may lead to "digital redlining," where some areas are left behind in terms of technological development and public investment.

Electric Vehicles (EVs): The adoption of EVs faces a similar hurdle. Despite falling prices, the upfront cost of EVs remains higher than that of traditional internal combustion engine vehicles. For many working-class families, the perceived economic burden outweighs the environmental benefits. Additionally, concerns about charging infrastructure, battery life, and the practicality of EVs in rural or remote areas add layers of scepticism.

2. Social and Cultural Resistance: Disruption of Traditional Lifestyles

While smart city initiatives and EV policies aim to create sustainable urban environments, they sometimes overlook the social and cultural dynamics of the communities they intend to serve.

Smart Cities: The shift towards smart city models can be seen as a top-down approach where decisions are made without meaningful community involvement. This can result in policies that feel disconnected from the lived experiences of residents. In cities like Barcelona and Toronto, community groups have voiced concerns about privacy, data ownership, and surveillance. They argue that smart city technologies often operate as "data extractors," capturing vast amounts of personal information without adequate transparency or consent.

In addition to privacy issues, there's a cultural resistance to the notion of "smart living." For some, the rapid digitalization of public spaces and services is seen as an imposition that disrupts traditional ways of life. In cities with rich historical or cultural identities, residents may view smart city developments as threats to their heritage, leading to tension between preservation and modernization.

Electric Vehicles: The push for EV adoption also faces cultural resistance, especially in regions where the automobile is more than just a mode of transport—it is a symbol of freedom, identity, and status. In parts of the United States, Australia, and Germany, where car culture is deeply ingrained, the shift to electric vehicles is seen as a challenge to these long-held values. Resistance comes not only from a reluctance to change but also from a perception that EV policies may be driven by elite urban agendas that do not align with rural or suburban lifestyles.

3. Environmental Concerns: Unintended Consequences

While smart cities and EVs are promoted as environmentally friendly solutions, some citizens and experts have raised questions about the true ecological impact of these technologies.

Smart Cities: Critics argue that the environmental benefits of smart city technologies can sometimes be overstated. For instance, the deployment of 5G networks, which is crucial for many smart city functions, involves a significant increase in energy consumption and electronic waste. Furthermore, the focus on high-tech solutions might overshadow simpler, more sustainable practices, such as urban green spaces, pedestrian-friendly infrastructure, and public transportation.

Electric Vehicles: EVs are often hailed as the future of sustainable transportation, but they are not without their ecological footprints. Concerns have been raised about the mining of rare earth metals for batteries, the carbon emissions associated with battery production, and the environmental costs of developing charging infrastructure. Moreover, in regions where electricity is still primarily generated from fossil fuels, the environmental benefits of EVs are diminished. Critics call for a more nuanced approach that includes developing clean energy sources, rather than relying solely on electrification as the solution.

4. Political and Ideological Opposition: The Question of Control

Underlying much of the pushback against smart cities and EV policies is a broader ideological debate about governance, autonomy, and control.

Smart Cities: Critics from across the political spectrum argue that smart city technologies concentrate power in the hands of large corporations and government entities, potentially leading to greater surveillance and loss of individual autonomy. Concerns about "surveillance capitalism" have been voiced by activists who see smart cities as a means for tech companies to collect data under the guise of improving public services. Additionally, there is apprehension about the centralization of control over urban infrastructure, which could lead to greater political and economic inequality.

Electric Vehicles: The pushback against EV policies often taps into broader political and ideological divides, particularly in regions where climate policy is a contentious issue. Some see the emphasis on EVs as a move by governments to dictate personal choices and behaviours, infringing upon individual freedoms. In countries where there is a strong political alignment with fossil fuel industries, EV policies are often framed as attacks on traditional energy sectors and local economies.

5. Grassroots Movements: Advocacy for Inclusive and Holistic Approaches

In response to the perceived shortcomings of smart city and EV policies, many grassroots movements have emerged advocating for more inclusive and community-driven approaches. These movements often emphasize the need for:

- **Local Participation and Transparency:** Advocates call for greater transparency in decision-making processes and more opportunities for community involvement in shaping the policies that affect them.
- **Equitable Distribution of Benefits:** There is a push for policies that ensure technological advancements benefit all segments of society, not just the affluent or tech-savvy.
- **Holistic Sustainability:** Instead of focusing solely on technological solutions, some groups advocate for a broader definition of sustainability that includes social justice, economic equality, and environmental stewardship.

Conclusion

The pushback against smart cities and EV policies highlights the complex and often contentious nature of urban transformation in the 21st century. While these initiatives promise significant benefits, they also present challenges that must be navigated thoughtfully and inclusively. For policymakers, urban planners, and technologists, the lesson is clear: creating a truly "smart" and sustainable future requires not only innovation but also engagement, equity, and empathy for the diverse needs and aspirations of all citizens.

Capital gains tax

The way I see it if Vice President Kamala Harris wins the next U.S. presidential election and moves forward with a policy to increase capital gains taxes, there could be several adverse impacts on the U.S. economy, particularly in the context of high inflation and a declining manufacturing sector and consequently our Canadian economy:

1. Reduced Investment Incentives Amid High Inflation

With inflation running high, investors are already looking for returns that exceed inflation to maintain their purchasing power. If capital gains taxes are increased, the after-tax return on investments diminishes, making such investments less attractive. This could lead to a decrease in the flow of capital into productive assets, which is critical in an inflationary environment where the value of money is eroding.

2. Potential Aggravation of Economic Decline in Manufacturing

A higher capital gains tax could further discourage investments in sectors like manufacturing, which are already experiencing a decline. Manufacturing requires substantial capital investment to innovate and modernize, but higher taxes could increase the cost of raising such capital. Without sufficient investment, the manufacturing sector's decline could deepen, leading to lower productivity, fewer jobs, and a slower economic recovery.

3. Negative Effects on Capital Formation and Reinvestment

Investors may be less likely to sell assets and reinvest in new opportunities if capital gains taxes are increased, particularly in struggling sectors like manufacturing. A decline in capital reinvestment can hinder the adoption of new technologies and the rejuvenation of ageing industries, which are essential for boosting productivity and economic growth.

4. Reduced Market Liquidity and Economic Dynamism

Higher capital gains taxes could lead to reduced trading activity, decreasing market liquidity. In an economy dealing with inflation and uncertainty, reduced liquidity could make it more challenging for businesses to access capital for expansion or restructuring. This could stifle economic dynamism and slow down recovery efforts.

In essence, if Vice President Harris's proposal to raise capital gains taxes were enacted under current economic conditions, it could lead to a decline in investment, exacerbate the downturn in manufacturing, and reduce the overall ability of the U.S. economy to recover and grow. Her policymakers would need to carefully consider these potential consequences and not ideology when crafting tax policy in such a challenging economic climate.

Ensuring Business Viability in a Challenging Economic Landscape: A Guide for Existing and New Businesses

Over the past few years, businesses—both established and emerging—have faced a daunting economic environment. Rising inflation, high interest rates, increasing crime, and the financial pressures related to illegal immigration have all contributed to a climate of uncertainty. For existing businesses and new start-ups alike, these factors demand a rethinking of traditional business strategies to ensure long-term viability.

The Impact of Inflation and Interest Rates

Inflation has significantly altered consumer behaviour, with many people tightening their belts and cutting non-essential spending. For existing businesses, this shift requires a reassessment of pricing strategies and cost structures. Meanwhile, start-ups must be particularly mindful of their pricing models, ensuring they offer value while staying competitive in a price-sensitive market.

High interest rates add another layer of complexity. Established businesses that have relied on credit to fuel growth or manage cash flow are now facing steeper borrowing costs. Startups, often reliant on external funding, are finding it more expensive to secure the capital needed to launch and scale. Both must now focus on efficient cash flow management and consider alternative funding sources, such as equity financing or strategic partnerships.

Addressing Security Concerns and Crime Costs

The rise in crime poses a significant risk to businesses of all sizes. For established businesses, the focus may need to shift toward protecting existing assets and operations, possibly by investing in enhanced security measures or insurance. Startups, on the other hand, should factor security costs into their initial business plans, understanding that the protection of their fledgling enterprise is crucial to survival and growth.

Whether it's retail theft, cybersecurity threats, or vandalism, businesses must be proactive. Established businesses might leverage their scale to negotiate better terms with security providers or invest in sophisticated technology. Startups, while possibly having fewer resources, can take advantage of newer, often more agile security solutions that are scalable as they grow.

Navigating the Complexities of Illegal Immigration

For existing businesses, particularly those in industries like agriculture, construction, or hospitality, the costs and complexities associated with illegal immigration are well known. These businesses may benefit from revisiting their labour strategies, perhaps by investing in automation or training programs that reduce dependence on low-wage labour.

Startups should carefully consider the implications of their workforce strategies from the outset. Understanding the local labour market, staying compliant with immigration laws, and anticipating potential policy changes can help avoid costly disruptions in the future. Startups may also explore innovative business models that reduce reliance on large, low-skilled labour forces, focusing instead on technology-driven solutions.

Strategies for Building Resilience

Given these challenges, both established businesses and start-ups need to prioritize resilience. For existing businesses, this might mean diversifying revenue streams, investing in technology to streamline operations, or even re-evaluating market focus to adapt to changing consumer behaviours.

Startups, with the advantage of a blank slate, can build flexibility into their business models from the ground up. By incorporating scenario planning into their strategies, they can better anticipate and adapt to economic shifts, whether that's further inflation, interest rate hikes, or changes in immigration policy.

For both types of businesses, prudent debt management is essential. Startups should be especially cautious about taking on too much debt in the early stages, focusing instead on building strong equity bases or exploring non-debt funding options. Existing businesses might look to restructure existing debt or optimize their capital structure to reduce interest burden.

Conclusion

In today's volatile economic environment, the viability of a business—whether well-established or just starting—hinges on its ability to adapt, innovate, and manage risk effectively. For existing businesses, this means reassessing and refining strategies in response to new challenges. For startups, it's about designing a business model that is robust enough to navigate uncertainty from the outset. By focusing on resilience, financial prudence, and proactive risk management, businesses of all sizes can position themselves not just to survive, but to thrive in the years ahead.

The illusion of price controls

Decided to stir the political pot with my take on one of the latest WTF moments from the US.

As Vice President Kamala Harris gears up for her presidential campaign, she has increasingly advocated for price controls as a key part of her economic platform. This move is not only ironic but also deeply concerning, considering that the Biden-Harris administration, through rampant government overspending, is largely responsible for the inflation crisis plaguing the nation. Now, in an attempt to mitigate the consequences of their fiscal policies, Harris proposes a solution that history has shown to be both ineffective and detrimental.

Inflation, at its core, is the result of an imbalance where too much money chases too few goods—often a direct consequence of excessive government spending. Under the Biden-Harris administration, federal expenditures have soared, leading to a significant increase in the money supply without a corresponding rise in economic output. This devaluation of currency has driven up prices, eroding the purchasing power of Americans, particularly those in lower-income brackets.

In response to the resulting economic pain, Vice President Harris has pushed for price controls as a remedy. However, history provides numerous examples of how such measures have consistently failed to address inflation and, in many cases, have exacerbated economic problems. A notable example is the experience of the United Kingdom in the 1970s under Prime Minister Harold Wilson's Labour government. Faced with rising inflation, Wilson implemented wage and price controls as part of his economic policy. Rather than stabilizing the economy, these controls led to widespread distortions, including shortages and a decline in the quality of goods. The British economy struggled under these artificial constraints, and inflation persisted, eventually contributing to a broader economic malaise that plagued the country throughout the decade.

The Soviet Union offers an even starker warning. The Soviet government's extensive price controls were a cornerstone of its centrally planned economy. Instead of fostering economic stability, these controls resulted in chronic shortages, inefficiencies, and a thriving black market. Producers, unable to profit under artificially low prices, reduced output or diverted goods to illicit markets, where they could be sold at much higher prices. This economic dysfunction was a significant factor in the eventual collapse of the Soviet system.

Similarly, in 301 AD, Roman Emperor Diocletian's" Edict on Maximum Prices ", was an attempt to control rampant inflation caused by the debasement of currency. (Caused by reducing the silver or gold content of the coinage). The edict set price ceilings on goods and services but failed to address the underlying economic issues. The result was widespread shortages, as producers could not afford to sell at the imposed prices, leading to the growth of black markets and further economic decline.

In the United States, the futility of price controls was evident in the 1970s under President Richard Nixon. Faced with rising inflation, Nixon imposed wage and price controls, which temporarily suppressed price increases but led to significant market distortions. Once the controls were lifted, inflation surged back even more aggressively, highlighting the failure to address the root causes—namely, government overspending and loose monetary policy.

Vice President Harris's proposal to implement price controls ignores these historical lessons. Rather than solving the inflation problem, such measures are likely to worsen it by distorting markets, creating shortages, and fueling black-market activities. More importantly, they fail to address the underlying cause of inflation: the excessive government spending that has occurred under the very administration in which she plays a central role.

In conclusion, Kamala Harris's advocacy for price controls is not only economically flawed but also deeply misguided. As part of the administration that has significantly contributed to the current inflation crisis through unchecked government spending, she now proposes socialist-style price controls that will not resolve the underlying issue but will instead exacerbate the economic situation. If Harris is serious about tackling inflation, she must first acknowledge the role she has played in creating it and pivot towards responsible fiscal policies, rather than relying on historically failed strategies that have consistently led to economic disaster.

Why Our Government Is Not Doing Its Job: My Thoughts on Current Policies

Inflation is eroding our purchasing power and making everyday life more expensive. In my view, the government's current policies are significantly to blame. Overspending, expenditures on illegal migrants, tax breaks and allowances for electric vehicle (EV) manufacturing, the suppression of the fossil fuel industry, and the push for digital bank currencies are all contributing to the problem. Furthermore, the unnecessary expenditures post-COVID and the unwarranted push for green technology do not reflect what Canadian citizens voted for.

Government Overspending

Government overspending is a major driver of inflation. When spending exceeds revenue, the government borrows more, which can push up interest rates. Higher interest rates mean higher costs for businesses and consumers, which businesses then pass on to us, driving prices up.

Moreover, excessive government spending increases the money supply. More money chasing the same amount of goods and services inevitably leads to higher prices. The expansive fiscal policies implemented during the COVID-19 pandemic, while necessary at the time, have significantly contributed to the inflation we're seeing today. The continuation of such spending post-COVID is unnecessary and exacerbates the issue.

Spending on Illegal Migrants

The government also spends substantial amounts on illegal migrants, providing healthcare, education, and social services. While I understand the humanitarian reasons behind this, it strains public finances and contributes to inflation.

The influx of illegal migrants affects the labour market by increasing competition for jobs, which can suppress wages and contribute to wage inflation in lower-income brackets. This dynamic further exacerbates overall inflation. It should be not allowed. Hence the term "Illegal".

Tax Breaks and Allowances for EV Manufacturing

While transitioning to green energy is deemed crucial by our Government, (Duh!), it's tax breaks and allowances for EV manufacturing distort the market. These incentives lower EV costs for consumers but require significant public funds, which adds to fiscal deficits and inflation. The rapid scaling up of EV production also leads to supply chain issues and higher raw material prices, driving up costs in related sectors. I have also mentioned in previous posts our inability to charge these EVs without significant cost.

Suppression of the Fossil Fuel Industry

To promote green technologies, the government is actively suppressing the fossil fuel industry through regulations and taxes. This suppression reduces the supply of fossil fuels, which leads to higher prices as demand remains steady or increases. Higher energy costs for oil, gas, transportation, heating, and electricity ripple through the economy, raising the cost of goods and services and contributing to inflation. This push for green technology is ill-intentioned, and not what Canadian citizens voted for and is contributing to economic instability.

Push for Digital Bank Currencies

The government's push for digital bank currencies represents another concerning development. While digital currencies can offer efficiencies, they also enable the government to exert greater control over the money supply. This control could lead to increased taxation and spending, further inflating the economy. Moreover, the potential for the government to take more direct action in the money supply raises serious concerns about financial autonomy and privacy for citizens.

My Conclusion

In conclusion, the government's current policies are failing to address inflation effectively. Overspending, expenditures on illegal migrants, incentives for EV manufacturing, the suppression of the fossil fuel industry, and the push for digital bank currencies are all contributing to the rising cost of living. Additionally, the unnecessary expenditure post-COVID and the unwarranted push for green technology do not reflect the will of Canadian citizens. It's clear that a more balanced approach is needed—one that promotes sustainable growth and environmental protection without causing economic instability. We need a government that must step up and navigate these challenges more effectively to mitigate inflation and ensure economic stability for all Canadian citizens and legal residents!

Part V: Navigating the Future of Urban Development

Can Smart Be Sustainable? Reimagining the Future of Cities

As urban populations continue to rise, cities around the world face unprecedented challenges in balancing growth, sustainability, and livability. The concept of the "smart city" has emerged as a promising solution to address these challenges by leveraging technology, data analytics, and innovation to optimize urban functions. However, the question remains: **Can smart cities also be sustainable?** In examining this question, we must consider alternative models and strategies that prioritize sustainable urban growth while embracing the technological advancements that characterize smart cities.

The Evolution of Smart Cities

The notion of a "smart city" has evolved significantly over the past few decades. Initially, it was synonymous with high-tech infrastructure and digital connectivity. Cities like Singapore, Barcelona, and Copenhagen pioneered the integration of information and communication technologies (ICT) to improve urban management, from traffic control to waste management. The goal was to create efficient, responsive, and resilient urban environments. Yet, as these models have matured, there has been a growing recognition that technological advancements alone are insufficient to create truly sustainable cities.

The Challenge of Sustainability

Sustainability in urban contexts goes beyond simply reducing carbon footprints or enhancing energy efficiency; it encompasses a holistic approach that includes economic viability, social equity, and environmental stewardship. The challenge lies in ensuring that smart city initiatives align with these broader sustainability goals. Often, smart cities have been criticized for prioritizing technological solutions over the needs of local communities, leading to increased inequality, privacy concerns, and even ecological degradation.

For example, smart city projects have sometimes focused on the deployment of sensors, data centres, and other infrastructure that require substantial energy and resources, offsetting the intended sustainability benefits. Moreover, the rapid pace of technological change can lead to obsolescence and waste, creating new environmental issues. Thus, the question arises: **How can cities balance being 'smart' with being 'sustainable'?**

Rethinking Smart Cities: Alternative Models for Sustainable Urban Growth

To reimagine the future of cities, it is essential to explore alternative models that prioritize sustainability alongside technological innovation. Here are some key strategies and models that can guide the development of smart and sustainable cities:

1. **Human-Centric Urban Design:** Cities should prioritize the needs and well-being of their inhabitants, focusing on human-centric design principles that enhance livability. This includes creating green spaces, promoting walkability, and ensuring access to essential services like healthcare, education, and public transportation. The concept of the "15-minute city," where all necessary amenities are within a 15-minute walk or bike ride from residents' homes, has gained traction as a sustainable model. It emphasizes compact, mixed-use urban development that reduces dependency on cars and promotes social cohesion.

2. **Circular Economy Approaches:** A sustainable city

minimizes waste and maximizes resource efficiency. Adopting a circular economy approach can help cities achieve this goal by designing systems that reuse, recycle, and regenerate resources. For instance, urban planning can integrate waste-to-energy systems, water recycling, and sustainable building materials to create a closed-loop system that reduces environmental impact. Cities like Amsterdam have already started implementing circular economy principles to create more sustainable urban environments.

3. **Decentralized and Resilient Energy Systems:** Traditional energy systems in cities are often centralized, making them vulnerable to disruptions and inefficiencies. Transitioning to decentralized energy systems that rely on renewable sources, such as solar, wind, and geothermal, can enhance sustainability. Microgrids, energy storage solutions, and community-driven renewable energy projects can empower local communities, reduce dependence on fossil fuels, and increase resilience against climate change impacts.

4. **Data for Good: Ethical and Inclusive Data Governance:** While data is a cornerstone of smart city initiatives, it is crucial to establish ethical frameworks for data governance that prioritize privacy, security, and inclusivity. Cities should implement transparent data-sharing policies and ensure that data is used to benefit all residents, not just private entities or specific demographics. Participatory data governance models can engage citizens in decision-making processes, ensuring that smart city projects are aligned with community needs and values.

5. **Nature-Based Solutions:** Incorporating nature-based solutions (NBS) into urban planning can help cities become more sustainable and resilient. NBS leverage natural processes and ecosystems to address urban challenges such as

air pollution, heat islands, and flood management. Examples include green roofs, urban forests, and wetlands that provide natural cooling, enhance biodiversity, and improve air quality. Cities like Singapore have successfully integrated NBS into their urban fabric, combining high-tech solutions with a commitment to maintaining and enhancing natural ecosystems.

6. **Collaborative Governance and Policy Innovation:** Sustainable urban growth requires innovative governance models that foster collaboration between governments, private sector players, academia, and civil society. Public-private partnerships, cross-sectoral coalitions, and community-driven initiatives can help bridge the gap between technological innovation and sustainability. Policymakers must also create regulatory frameworks that encourage sustainable practices, from green building codes to incentives for renewable energy adoption.

Case Studies: Examples of Smart and Sustainable Cities

Several cities around the world have made strides in balancing smart city initiatives with sustainability. For example:

- **Freiburg, Germany:** Known as the "Green City," Freiburg has implemented a comprehensive sustainability plan that integrates renewable energy, green mobility, and eco-friendly urban development. It has a strong focus on citizen participation and has developed a model for a low-carbon, high-quality urban life.
- **Curitiba, Brazil:** This city is celebrated for its innovative and sustainable urban planning, particularly its efficient public transportation system, green spaces, and waste management

programs. Curitiba demonstrates how smart solutions can be developed with an emphasis on social equity and environmental stewardship.

- **Melbourne, Australia:** Melbourne is integrating smart city technologies with sustainability goals, such as optimizing water usage through smart sensors and expanding green infrastructure. The city has also embraced the concept of the 20-minute neighbourhood to reduce car dependency and promote local economies.

The Future of Cities: Smart, Sustainable, and Equitable

The future of cities lies in their ability to harmonize technological innovation with sustainability principles. Smart cities have the potential to address some of the most pressing urban challenges of our time, from climate change to social inequality. However, achieving this potential requires a paradigm shift—from a technology-centric approach to a more holistic model that integrates environmental sustainability, social inclusivity, and economic resilience.

As cities continue to grow and evolve, embracing alternative models and strategies for sustainable urban growth will be essential. The answer to whether "smart" can be "sustainable" lies not in the technology itself but in how we choose to deploy it—thoughtfully, inclusively, and with a long-term vision for a better urban future.

Beyond the Grid: Future Technologies and Decentralized Solutions

Exploring Technological Advancements that Could Provide Alternative Solutions for Energy and Mobility

In an era marked by rapid technological innovation, the quest for sustainable and efficient energy and mobility solutions has taken centre stage. Traditional centralized energy systems, which rely heavily on large power plants and extensive grid infrastructure, face significant challenges. These challenges include ageing infrastructure, vulnerability to natural disasters and cyberattacks, and growing demand for cleaner and more decentralized energy sources. As we move towards a future where energy needs to be both sustainable and resilient, decentralized solutions and emerging technologies are poised to play a pivotal role.

This article explores some of the most promising advancements in energy and mobility technologies that are pushing us "beyond the grid" and towards a more decentralized, efficient, and sustainable future.

1. Decentralized Energy Systems: Microgrids and Smart Grids

One of the most significant shifts in energy infrastructure is the move from centralized grids to more decentralized systems. At the forefront of this transition are **microgrids**—localized grids that can operate independently or in conjunction with larger grids. Microgrids provide several advantages: they increase resilience against outages, reduce transmission losses, and can integrate renewable energy sources like solar and wind more efficiently.

Alongside microgrids, **smart grids** are transforming how energy is distributed and consumed. Equipped with sensors, smart meters, and advanced analytics, smart grids enable real-time monitoring, demand response, and efficient energy distribution. This digital transformation of the energy grid allows for better integration of distributed energy resources (DERs), such as solar panels, wind turbines, and energy storage systems, which can be installed at the local or even household level.

These advancements facilitate a more responsive and adaptive energy system that can balance supply and demand dynamically, integrate renewable energy sources, and ensure more reliable energy delivery.

2. Renewable Energy Technologies: Solar, Wind, and

Beyond

Renewable energy technologies continue to evolve rapidly, offering more efficient, affordable, and scalable solutions for decentralized power generation. **Solar power**, for instance, has seen significant advancements in photovoltaic (PV) efficiency and cost reduction. Emerging technologies such as **perovskite solar cells** and **bifacial solar panels** promise even greater efficiency and flexibility in deployment.

Similarly, **wind energy** has benefited from innovations in turbine design, materials, and placement strategies. Floating offshore wind farms, for example, can harness stronger and more consistent winds found at sea, providing a substantial increase in energy generation potential.

Beyond these well-established renewables, other technologies like **ocean energy** (including tidal and wave power), **geothermal energy**, and **hydrogen fuel cells** are being explored as part of a diversified and decentralized energy mix. These technologies, particularly hydrogen, offer significant potential for energy storage and long-distance transport, making them vital for a sustainable energy future.

3. Energy Storage and Management: The Key to Decentralization

For decentralized energy systems to function effectively, reliable and efficient **energy storage** solutions are crucial. Energy storage not only bridges the gap between intermittent renewable energy generation and demand but also enhances grid stability and flexibility.

Lithium-ion batteries have been the dominant energy storage technology, but they are not without limitations, including resource scarcity, recycling challenges, and potential safety concerns. Consequently, research is expanding into alternative storage technologies such as **solid-state batteries**, **flow batteries**, and **compressed air energy storage (CAES)**.

Advanced energy management systems using artificial intelligence (AI) and machine learning (ML) are also gaining traction. These systems optimize energy production, storage, and consumption by analyzing vast amounts of data from various sources, predicting demand patterns, and automating decision-making processes.

4. Decentralized Mobility Solutions: The Rise of Autonomous and Electric Vehicles

As the energy landscape evolves, so too does the realm of mobility. The future of transportation is increasingly electric, autonomous, and decentralized. **Electric vehicles (EVs)** are at the forefront of this transformation, offering cleaner alternatives to internal combustion engine vehicles and creating opportunities for decentralized energy solutions.

Innovations in **battery technology**, such as **solid-state batteries** and **ultra-fast charging systems**, are addressing the limitations of current EVs, such as range anxiety and long charging times. Moreover, **vehicle-to-grid (V2G)** technology allows EVs to act as decentralized energy storage units, providing additional flexibility and stability to the grid.

Autonomous vehicles (AVs), powered by advancements in AI, sensors, and connectivity, are also set to redefine mobility. When combined with **shared mobility solutions**—such as autonomous shuttles and ride-sharing networks—AVs can significantly reduce the number of vehicles on the road, lower emissions, and optimize energy use in urban environments.

5. Blockchain and Decentralized Energy Markets

Blockchain technology is emerging as a powerful tool for enabling decentralized energy markets. By providing a secure, transparent, and immutable ledger for energy transactions, **blockchain** facilitates peer-to-peer (P2P) energy trading among consumers and producers.

This approach allows households with solar panels or wind turbines to sell excess energy directly to their neighbours, bypassing traditional utility companies and reducing energy costs.

Moreover, blockchain-based **smart contracts** can automate and streamline complex transactions, such as demand response programs, carbon credit trading, and renewable energy certificates, making energy markets more efficient and accessible.

6. The Role of Artificial Intelligence and IoT in Decentralized Solutions

The integration of **artificial intelligence (AI)** and the **Internet of Things (IoT)** into decentralized energy and mobility systems is a game-changer. AI algorithms can optimize energy production, consumption, and distribution, enhancing grid efficiency and stability. IoT devices, such as smart meters and sensors, provide real-time data that AI systems can analyze to predict energy demand and manage supply dynamically.

In the mobility sector, AI and IoT are crucial for enabling **connected vehicle ecosystems**, where vehicles communicate with each other and with infrastructure to optimize traffic flow, reduce congestion, and enhance safety. This convergence of technologies supports the development of **smart cities**, where decentralized energy and mobility solutions work in harmony to create more sustainable and efficient urban environments.

7. Challenges and Opportunities

While the future of decentralized energy and mobility systems is promising, several challenges must be addressed to realize their full potential. **Regulatory frameworks** need to evolve to support decentralized energy markets, protect consumer rights, and ensure data privacy and security. Moreover, the integration of diverse energy sources and technologies requires robust standards and interoperability.

Investment in research and development is also critical to advancing emerging technologies and making them commercially viable. Public and private sector collaboration will be essential to overcome these barriers and drive the adoption of decentralized solutions.

Conclusion: A Future Beyond the Grid

The future of energy and mobility is undoubtedly moving beyond the grid. Decentralized solutions, powered by renewable energy, advanced storage technologies, smart grids, and AI-driven systems, are transforming how we produce, distribute, and consume energy. As we continue to innovate and integrate these technologies, we could build a more sustainable, resilient, and equitable energy future that empowers communities and reduces our reliance on centralized, fossil fuel-based systems.

By embracing these advancements and addressing the challenges ahead, we can pave the way for a decentralized energy and mobility landscape that benefits not only our economies but also the planet and future generations.

A New Urban Compact: Balancing Innovation, Sustainability, and Human Needs

The 21st century has ushered in an era of rapid urbanization, technological advancement, and evolving societal expectations. Cities worldwide are becoming more densely populated and interconnected, necessitating a fundamental rethinking of urban development. Traditional models, with their singular focus on either economic growth or technological progress, have often overlooked the broader needs of sustainability and human-centric design. To foster cities that are truly livable and resilient, a new urban compact is needed—one that balances innovation, sustainability, and human needs.

1. The Need for a New Urban Compact

The urban landscape is undergoing unprecedented transformations. By 2050, it is projected that nearly 70% of the world's population will reside in urban areas, creating immense pressure on existing infrastructure, resources, and social services. As cities continue to expand, the challenges of climate change, inequality, and resource depletion are becoming more pronounced. Cities are responsible for over 70% of global carbon emissions, and their sprawling, car-dependent designs often exacerbate social inequalities.

Traditional urban planning approaches, which prioritize economic growth or technological advancement above all else, are increasingly proving inadequate. A new paradigm—one that seamlessly integrates technological innovation, sustainable practices, and human-centred design principles—is essential to developing future cities that are resilient, inclusive, and sustainable.

2. The Role of Innovation in Urban Development

Innovation, driven by technology, has the potential to transform cities into smarter, more efficient environments. Smart cities, leveraging the Internet of Things (IoT), artificial intelligence (AI), and big data analytics, are optimizing urban management. From intelligent transportation systems that reduce congestion and emissions to smart grids that ensure efficient energy use, technology offers a pathway to better urban living.

However, innovation must be pursued thoughtfully. Technology should not be the end goal but rather a means to enhance the quality of life. For instance, urban innovation should focus on solving critical problems like affordable housing, efficient public transportation, and waste management. Emerging technologies such as autonomous vehicles, AI-driven urban planning, and smart infrastructure must align with broader social and environmental objectives.

A balanced approach recognizes that innovation must be adaptable, inclusive, and responsive to the evolving needs of urban residents. Instead of deploying technology for technology's sake, cities must prioritize solutions that enhance livability, equity, and resilience.

3. Sustainability as the Cornerstone of Urban Planning

Sustainability must be at the heart of any new urban compact. Future cities must be designed to minimize their environmental footprint while maximizing the well-being of their inhabitants. This involves a shift towards more sustainable urban planning models that emphasize resource efficiency, renewable energy, and green infrastructure.

Key elements of sustainable urban design include:

- **Compact and Mixed-Use Development:** To reduce reliance on automobiles and lower emissions, cities should encourage higher-density, mixed-use development that integrates residential, commercial, and recreational spaces within walkable distances.

- **Green and Blue Infrastructure:** Incorporating green spaces, urban forests, and water bodies not only enhances biodiversity but also improves air quality, mitigates urban heat islands, and offers recreational spaces for residents.

- **Circular Economy Principles:** Cities should transition from a linear "take-make-dispose" model to a circular economy, where resources are reused, recycled, and repurposed, reducing waste and conserving natural resources.

- **Renewable Energy and Smart Grids:** Investing in renewable energy sources such as solar, wind, and geothermal, coupled with smart grids, can significantly reduce a city's carbon footprint while enhancing energy security.

Sustainable cities are not only more environmentally friendly but also more resilient to shocks, such as natural disasters, pandemics, and economic downturns. A focus on sustainability ensures that cities remain livable and thriving for generations to come.

4. Human-Centric Design: Putting People at the Core

While innovation and sustainability are critical components of future cities, they must be balanced with a strong emphasis on human-centric design. Cities are, after all, for people. A human-centric approach to urban planning considers the needs, desires, and well-being of all residents, fostering inclusivity, accessibility, and equity.

Human-centric design involves:

- **Public Spaces and Social Interaction:** Urban spaces should promote social interaction, community building, and cultural expression. This involves creating accessible public spaces, such as parks, plazas, and community centres, that cater to diverse social, cultural, and recreational needs.
- **Affordable and Inclusive Housing:** Cities should provide affordable, diverse, and inclusive housing options that cater to people of all income levels. This includes mixed-income housing, cooperative housing, and policies that prevent displacement and gentrification.
- **Walkability and Public Transport:** Prioritizing pedestrian-friendly streets, cycling paths, and efficient public transport systems reduces the dependence on private vehicles and promotes healthier, more connected communities.
- **Health and Well-being:** Urban design should prioritize residents' physical and mental health by ensuring access to

healthcare, recreational facilities, green spaces, and clean air and water.

By prioritizing the human experience, cities can foster environments where residents feel safe, valued, and empowered to thrive.

5. Achieving Balance: The Way Forward

Achieving a balanced approach to urban development requires a shift in mindset, governance, and policy. Collaboration between governments, private sector players, civil society, and citizens is essential. Policymakers must adopt a holistic approach that integrates technological innovation, sustainable practices, and human-centric principles into a cohesive urban strategy.

Some key actions for achieving this balance include:

- **Inclusive Governance and Citizen Participation:** Urban planning should be a participatory process that involves all stakeholders, including marginalized communities. Inclusive governance ensures that the voices of all residents are heard and that urban policies reflect diverse needs and perspectives.
- **Cross-Sector Collaboration:** Governments, businesses, and non-profit organizations must collaborate to develop and implement integrated urban solutions. Public-private partnerships can accelerate innovation and investment in sustainable infrastructure.
- **Policy and Regulatory Frameworks:** Governments must develop robust policy and regulatory frameworks that incentivize sustainable practices, regulate the deployment of new technologies, and ensure equitable access to urban amenities.

Conclusion

The future of cities lies in their ability to innovate, sustain, and care for their inhabitants. A new urban compact, grounded in a balanced approach that integrates technological innovation, sustainability, and human-centric design, can pave the way for cities that are not only smart and green but also inclusive and resilient. As we stand at the crossroads of urban evolution, it is imperative to reimagine our cities as places where people, nature, and technology coexist harmoniously—creating a sustainable, prosperous, and equitable future for all.

The Road Ahead: Preparing for an Uncertain Urban Future

The future of urban environments is fraught with uncertainty, marked by rapid technological advances, climate change, economic shifts, and unprecedented demographic transformations. As cities worldwide grapple with the multifaceted challenges that lie ahead, the imperative to build resilient, adaptable, and sustainable urban environments becomes ever more urgent. This article explores the key issues shaping the future of urban living and outlines strategies for cities, citizens, and policymakers to navigate these uncertainties.

The Drivers of Urban Uncertainty

Several driving forces will shape the future of urban landscapes:

1. **Climate Change and Environmental Stressors**: Rising temperatures, extreme weather events, sea-level rise, and resource scarcity are some of the most pressing issues that cities will face. Urban areas, particularly coastal cities, are on

the front lines of climate change, needing both immediate and long-term adaptation strategies to mitigate risks.

2. **Technological Disruption**: Emerging technologies such as artificial intelligence (AI), the Internet of Things (IoT), and autonomous transportation promise to reshape urban life profoundly. These technologies can enhance urban management and improve service delivery but also pose challenges around privacy, data security, and the displacement of traditional jobs.

3. **Demographic Shifts and Urbanization**: The rapid urbanization trend, especially in developing nations, coupled with ageing populations in many developed countries, presents unique challenges. Cities will need to accommodate growing populations, provide affordable housing, and ensure equitable access to services while also catering to the needs of older residents.

4. **Economic Uncertainty and Inequality**: Economic volatility, globalization, and rising inequality threaten urban cohesion and stability. Many cities face growing disparities in wealth, access to quality education, healthcare, and employment opportunities. Addressing these inequalities is crucial to maintaining social harmony and fostering inclusive growth.

5. **Public Health and Pandemics**: The COVID-19 pandemic highlighted the vulnerabilities of urban centres to public health crises. Future pandemics or health emergencies could further strain healthcare systems, disrupt economies, and challenge urban governance structures, underscoring the need for robust public health infrastructure and response plans.

Strategies for Adaptation and Resilience

To prepare for the uncertain road ahead, cities, citizens, and policymakers must adopt a forward-thinking, collaborative, and integrated approach. Below are some strategies to build resilience and adaptability:

1. Building Climate-Resilient Cities

To tackle the impending challenges posed by climate change, cities must invest in green infrastructure, sustainable urban planning, and resilient building designs. This could include creating urban green spaces, implementing flood defences, improving public transportation, and adopting renewable energy sources. Cities should also engage in comprehensive climate risk assessments to better understand and plan for future vulnerabilities.

2. Leveraging Technology for Smart Urban Management

Embracing smart city technologies can revolutionize urban management, making cities more efficient, responsive, and sustainable. AI and IoT can optimize energy use, reduce traffic congestion, enhance public safety, and monitor environmental quality in real-time. However, urban planners must ensure that technology deployment is inclusive, transparent, and accountable, with robust data protection measures to safeguard citizen privacy.

3. Fostering Social Equity and Inclusion

Urban resilience is not just about physical infrastructure but also about social cohesion and inclusivity. Policymakers must prioritize affordable housing, access to quality education, and equitable healthcare services to bridge the growing divide between different urban populations.

Community-driven development, participatory planning, and inclusive decision-making can help build a more equitable urban future.

4. Promoting Sustainable Economic Growth

Cities need to foster sustainable economic models that create inclusive growth opportunities for all citizens. This includes supporting small and medium-sized enterprises (SMEs), promoting green jobs, and investing in digital skills and training to prepare the workforce for future industries. Encouraging public-private partnerships and fostering innovation ecosystems can also drive economic resilience in uncertain times.

5. Strengthening Urban Governance and Policy Integration

Urban governance must become more agile and adaptable to respond to dynamic and evolving challenges. This requires integrated planning across sectors, levels of government, and geographic scales. Policies must be flexible, data-driven, and evidence-based, incorporating input from diverse stakeholders, including citizens, businesses, academia, and civil society.

6. Enhancing Public Health and Preparedness

Building robust public health infrastructure, including early warning systems, effective emergency response plans, and accessible healthcare services, is critical to urban resilience. Lessons from the COVID-19 pandemic should inform future preparedness strategies, emphasizing the need for collaborative efforts between cities, regions, and international organizations to tackle health crises.

Concluding Thoughts: Embracing a Future of Uncertainty with Adaptation and Innovation

The road ahead for urban environments is undoubtedly challenging, but it is also filled with opportunities for innovation, collaboration, and transformation. Cities, citizens, and policymakers must embrace an adaptive mindset, recognizing that uncertainty is not just a challenge but also a catalyst for change.

Building resilient, sustainable, and inclusive cities requires a multi-dimensional approach that integrates technological innovation, equitable policies, climate adaptation, and robust governance frameworks. Citizens must be empowered to actively participate in shaping their urban futures, while policymakers need to foster a culture of collaboration, transparency, and inclusivity.

Ultimately, the cities that thrive in an uncertain future will be those that are willing to reimagine, reinvent, and reinvest in their urban environments—embracing change as an opportunity to build better, more resilient communities for all.

Part VI: "Sustainable Cities or State Control? The Future of Urban Living Under Government Mandates"

The Growing Disconnect Between Western Governments and Their Electorates

In recent years, a troubling trend has emerged across Western democracies: an increasing disconnect between the policies of elected governments and the will of the people who voted them into office. From the issues of illegal migration to mandates on electric vehicles (EVs) and the erosion of free speech, a pattern is clear: many Western governments seem more aligned with technocratic agendas and elite interests than with the everyday concerns of their citizens. This divergence is not only fueling public dissatisfaction but is also reminiscent of the dystopian warnings of George Orwell's *1984*, where truth and freedom are sacrificed for power and control.

The Issue of Illegal Migration

One of the most contentious issues facing Western societies today is the seemingly unchecked flow of illegal migration. Despite repeated polling that shows significant portions of the electorate are concerned about this issue—often citing economic strain, cultural integration challenges, and security risks—governments continue to allow, and in some cases even encourage, the influx of migrants. This is not to disregard the humanitarian aspect of migration; there are indeed cases where asylum is warranted. However, the lack of a clear and enforced legal framework for migration has left many citizens feeling that their concerns are being ignored.

Governments and institutions often dismiss these concerns as xenophobic or reactionary, but this simplification overlooks the genuine worries of working-class citizens who see their communities changing rapidly without their consent. It also neglects the economic realities of job competition, pressure on social services, and housing shortages. The political elites, insulated from these impacts, fail to recognize the gap between their rhetoric of inclusivity and the everyday realities faced by their constituents.

The Push for Electric Vehicle Mandates

A similar disconnect can be seen in the aggressive push for electric vehicle mandates. While there is broad consensus on the need to address climate change, the methods of achieving these goals are where the divergence begins. Governments in the West have set ambitious targets for phasing out internal combustion engines in favour of electric vehicles—targets that many experts argue are neither realistic nor feasible given current technological and infrastructural limitations.

Polls consistently show that while citizens may support environmental initiatives, there is a clear resistance to policies perceived as impractical or economically burdensome. The middle and lower classes, who rely on affordable and reliable transportation, see these mandates as punitive measures that disproportionately affect them. Meanwhile, policymakers, often with the backing of large corporations that stand to benefit from the green transition, continue to push these mandates without sufficient planning or consideration for the economic fallout.

The Erosion of Free Speech and Democratic Accountability

The most concerning aspect of this growing divide between government and the electorate is the increasing tendency to stifle dissent. Across the West, we are witnessing a surge in efforts to limit free speech, often under the guise of combating misinformation or hate speech. While some regulation is necessary to prevent harm, there is a fine line between safeguarding public discourse and controlling it. As in Orwell's *1984*, the control of information becomes a means of controlling thought.

The use of technology and social media platforms to silence or de-platform those with dissenting opinions, whether they are journalists, academics, or ordinary citizens, reflects a troubling trend. Governments, sometimes in collusion with tech giants, appear more interested in curating a "safe" public discourse than fostering a genuine marketplace of ideas. This has led to a growing perception that Western democracies are becoming less democratic, prioritizing ideological conformity over the values of free speech and open debate.

Why Are Governments Ignoring the Public?

The question arises: why are Western governments increasingly disregarding public opinion? The answer may lie in a combination of factors, including ideological capture, economic interests, and a belief in technocratic governance. Many in positions of power have become disconnected from the lives of ordinary citizens, instead aligning with globalist ideals that prioritize abstract concepts like "global governance" and "international cooperation" over national sovereignty and local needs.

Moreover, there is an economic dimension to consider. Policies on migration, climate, and technology often benefit large corporations and financial institutions that have significant influence over political decision-making. This influence, often described as "regulatory capture," leads to a scenario where governments are more responsive to the interests of a powerful minority than to most of their electorate.

The Need for Reconnecting with the Electorate

If Western democracies are to survive and thrive, a course correction is needed. Governments must prioritize reconnecting with their citizens, listening to their concerns, and formulating policies that are both effective and equitable. This requires moving away from technocratic governance and re-embracing the principles of representative democracy.

Moreover, protecting free speech and fostering open debate should be at the heart of this effort. Citizens need to feel that their voices matter and that they can express their concerns without fear of censorship or reprisal. Only by restoring trust between the governed and the governors can Western democracies hope to overcome the growing chasm that threatens their very foundations.

In conclusion, the increasing disconnect between Western governments and their populations is not just a political issue—it is a fundamental challenge to the democratic ideals upon which these societies are built. The time has come for a return to governance that truly represents the will of the people, rather than the will of a disconnected elite. Failure to do so risks not only political instability but the erosion of the freedoms that have defined Western civilization for centuries.

The Cost of Illegal Immigration: Crime, Cultural Clashes, and the Need for Strict Enforcement

As nations across the globe confront a surge in illegal and unvetted immigration, we are witnessing a troubling trend: a rise in migrant crime that mirrors this unchecked influx. This is not merely a debate about numbers or border policy—it's about the fundamental integrity of our societies and the steep costs we incur when we fail to enforce immigration laws and protect our shared values. The situation demands urgent and decisive action, and it is time for an unflinching examination of the economic, social, and cultural toll illegal immigration from third-world countries is taking on host nations. However, a critical question arises: Why are governments seemingly promoting or accepting this situation despite its clear costs and risks?

The Economic Burden of Illegal Immigration

The economic impact of illegal immigration is substantial and growing. Taxpayers bear the brunt of increased spending on law enforcement, healthcare, welfare, and social services to accommodate the rising numbers of undocumented immigrants. These costs are not just abstract figures; they represent a real strain on public resources that could otherwise be invested in the well-being of citizens and legal immigrants who contribute positively to society. When public schools become overcrowded, when healthcare systems are overwhelmed, and when welfare programs are stretched thin, it is evident that unchecked immigration imposes a significant financial burden.

Illegal immigration also distorts labour markets. When undocumented immigrants are willing to work for lower wages, it undercuts native workers and erodes fair labour practices. This creates economic instability for working-class families and disrupts job market dynamics. Given these clear economic harms, one must ask: Why do governments continue to allow this imbalance to persist? Is it a case of misplaced humanitarianism, political expediency, or something more deliberate?

The Rising Tide of Migrant Crime

One of the most concerning consequences of illegal, unvetted immigration is the corresponding rise in crime. While it is essential to recognize that not all migrants engage in criminal behaviour, data from numerous countries show a disproportionate involvement of certain migrant groups in crimes, ranging from theft and drug trafficking to violent offences. This pattern is not coincidental but a predictable outcome when individuals enter a country without adequate background checks or vetting.

Communities across Europe and North America have seen crime rates rise in parallel with waves of illegal immigration from countries where social and cultural norms differ significantly. Many migrants come from regions where the rule of law is weak, corruption is endemic, and crime is often a means of survival. This reality creates an environment where respect for the laws and values of the host country is not guaranteed but rather an exception. The question, then, is why governments continue to permit unregulated migration that brings such risks. Are they ignoring these patterns, or do they have other motives that override concerns about public safety?

Cultural Clashes and the Erosion of Shared Values

The challenges extend beyond economics and crime; they are also deeply cultural. An influx of migrants from regions with fundamentally different values and norms leads to a clash of civilizations. The foundational principles of Western democracies—such as freedom of expression, gender equality, secular governance, and individual rights—are often at odds with the beliefs held by many migrants from the developing world. When large numbers of migrants with differing values arrive, the potential for social discord escalates.

This divergence in values has real-world implications. We see the formation of parallel societies where migrant communities resist integration and instead create enclaves that defy the cultural norms of the host country. This phenomenon undermines social cohesion and threatens the concept of a unified nation based on shared values and responsibilities. If a country's core principles are not respected, the idea of national unity becomes untenable. Here, too, one must ask: Why are governments seemingly indifferent to this erosion of shared values? Are they prioritizing diversity over unity, or is there an ideological agenda at play?

The Need for Strict Enforcement and Value-Based Integration

To safeguard their economies, citizens, and cultural identity, countries must adopt a firmer stance on immigration. This begins with strict enforcement of immigration laws, robust border security, and comprehensive vetting processes to ensure only those who share—or are willing to adopt—the host country's values are allowed entry. While the right to asylum must be protected, it should not be exploited as a loophole for those who do not qualify.

Integration is another critical element, but it cannot be a one-sided effort. It is insufficient to provide language classes and job training;

immigrants must also be prepared to adopt the core values of the host society. Policies should encourage value-based integration, making it clear that adherence to local laws, customs, and social norms is a prerequisite for full participation in society.

A Call for Pragmatic, Value-Driven Immigration Policy

The rise in migrant crime, the economic strain of illegal immigration, and the erosion of shared societal values make it clear that a lax approach to immigration is unsustainable. Nations must regain control of their borders and futures by enacting policies that protect their citizens and preserve their foundational principles.

But the lingering question remains: Why are so many governments either promoting or accepting this situation, given its clear costs and risks? Is it due to a failure of leadership, a misguided adherence to political correctness, or a deeper ideological commitment to multiculturalism at any cost? These are the questions citizens must demand answers to as they seek leaders willing to prioritize the well-being, safety, and shared values of their people over abstract ideals and political expediency.

The stakes are simply too high for anything less than a resolute and rational approach to immigration.

The Role of Unchecked Illegal Immigration in Today's Crisis

Adding to these economic and fiscal challenges is the destabilization caused by unchecked illegal immigration, a problem that has been largely ignored or even tacitly encouraged by some of these left-leaning governments. In the United States, for example, the Biden-Harris administration's relaxed immigration policies have led to a significant increase in illegal crossings at the southern border. This has placed immense strain on local economies, public services, and law enforcement agencies, exacerbating social tensions and diverting resources from other critical areas. The potential new Government led by Harris will continue these policies and align with her stated views on price controls, etc., which could well bring ruination to the country.

In Canada, the Trudeau government has similarly faced criticism for its handling of immigration, with opponents arguing that the country's generous asylum policies have been exploited, leading to an influx of undocumented migrants. This has led to overcrowded housing, pressure on social services, and growing public discontent, particularly in provinces already struggling with economic challenges.

In the United Kingdom, illegal immigration has become a major political issue, with the new Labour government facing increasing pressure to address the problem. However, the Labour Party is advocating for more compassionate immigration policies, whilst critics argue that this approach fails to address the underlying issues of security, economic sustainability, and social cohesion. The situation has only worsened in recent years, with illegal migrants crossing the English Channel in record numbers, leading to a humanitarian crisis and growing public outcry.

The Dangers of History Repeating Itself

The lesson from Harold Wilson's Labour government is that extensive state intervention, while sometimes necessary, must be approached with caution. Nationalization, increased public spending, price controls and currency manipulation can have dire consequences if not carefully managed. The economic decline that Britain experienced in the 1970s was solely due to Wilson's policies being a significant contributing factor.

Today's left-leaning governments in the West must heed this historical lesson. While addressing social inequality, modernizing infrastructure, and combating climate change are noble goals, they must be balanced with sound economic management. Moreover, the failure to control illegal immigration adds another layer of complexity, threatening to destabilize economies, strain public services, and exacerbate social tensions. Otherwise, the risk is that history will repeat itself, with today's policies leading to tomorrow's economic crisis.

In conclusion, the comparison between Harold Wilson's Labour government and contemporary left-leaning administrations is more than a historical curiosity; it is a cautionary tale. The rise of state intervention increased public spending, and disregard for fiscal prudence, coupled with the destabilizing effects of unchecked illegal immigration, may resonate with the electorate, but they come with significant risks. As history has shown, the road to economic ruin is often paved with good intentions—and the added pressure of uncontrolled immigration may only hasten that journey.

The Real Cost of Unchecked Illegal Migration: The Way I See It

In recent years, the issue of illegal migration has become a hot topic, and while I understand the humanitarian concerns, I believe it's essential to look at the financial implications and how they affect a government's ability to serve its citizens. Unfortunately, it seems that some governments view illegal immigrants as a potential voting bloc to keep themselves in power, diverting resources away from those they were elected to represent.

The Financial Burden of Illegal Migration

From my perspective, governments operate on limited resources, primarily funded by the taxes paid by citizens and legal residents. When these funds are diverted to support illegal migrants—through healthcare, education, and social services—governments have to stretch their budgets further to maintain the same level of services for their actual citizens. This often results in higher taxes, increased borrowing, and cuts to essential services.

Take healthcare, for example. Providing services to illegal migrants imposes significant costs. Hospitals and clinics can become overwhelmed, leading to longer wait times and reduced quality of care for citizens like us. Last time in emergency I waited 14 hours and noted fully half the patients there did not speak either English or French and had no Insurance. In public schools, the situation is similar resources are already stretched thin, and when schools must accommodate the children of illegal migrants, it can lead to overcrowded classrooms, overworked teachers, and a decline in the quality of education for all students.

The Hidden Agenda: A Potential Voting Bloc

I can't help but feel that some governments are looking at illegal migrants as a potential voting bloc. By providing support and creating pathways to citizenship for these individuals, it seems they're trying to secure their political future. This strategy is not only unsustainable but also unfair to the rest of us. We pay our taxes with the expectation that the government will use those funds to improve our quality of life—not to pursue a political agenda designed to keep certain parties in power.

When governments prioritize the interests of a potential new voter base over the needs of their current citizens, they undermine the social contract and erode public trust. It feels like our needs are being sidelined in favour of a strategy that ultimately serves the government more than the people.

The Impact on Public Services

I see how this strain on public services affects all of us, especially the most vulnerable. Public services like healthcare and education are already under pressure in many places, and when governments divert resources to support illegal migrants, it leaves even less for the rest of us. This can lead to a decline in the quality of care in hospitals, longer wait times, and overcrowded classrooms in schools.

It's not just about inconvenience—it's about fairness. Seniors, low-income families, and others who rely heavily on public services are the ones who suffer the most when resources are stretched thin. They might find it harder to access the healthcare they need, or their children might not get the quality education they deserve. And all of this is happening because governments are diverting resources that should be used to serve their citizens.

The Need for a Balanced Approach

Addressing illegal migration is complex, and I know there's no easy solution. However, I believe governments must prioritize the needs of their citizens first. This means enforcing immigration laws, making sure public services are adequately funded, and allocating resources in a way that reflects the will of the people—not just the interests of those trying to secure their political future.

I'm not saying we should turn our backs on those in need, but there has to be a balance. Stricter immigration policies, better border security, and more rigorous enforcement of existing laws are necessary. By doing this, governments can ensure they have the resources to provide high-quality public services to citizens like us without compromising financial stability.

Conclusion

The way I see it, unchecked illegal migration places an unsustainable financial burden on governments and, ultimately, on us—the citizens who fund these governments through our taxes. While helping those in need is important, it has to be balanced with the responsibility to provide for the citizens who rely on government services. The solution lies in a balanced approach that enforces immigration laws while ensuring that public services remain robust and well-funded for those who are legally entitled to them. Only then can governments truly fulfil their duty to serve us, the people who elected them, rather than courting a potential new voting bloc.

Opinion: Who Truly Bears the Cost of Government Policies on EVs, Immigration, and Spending?

Western governments have increasingly embraced policies centred on electric vehicles (EVs), open immigration, and massive government spending, all of which are presented as progressive solutions to environmental, economic, and social challenges. Proponents argue that these policies are necessary for the future—cleaner air, more robust economies, and more inclusive societies. However, a closer examination reveals that these policies come with substantial costs, often borne by ordinary citizens. Moreover, there is a case to be made that the significant misuse of taxpayer revenues for these initiatives could be better deployed elsewhere for the collective benefit of society.

Immigration: Economic Necessity or Social Strain?

Western nations have also embraced immigration as a strategy to address declining birth rates, labour shortages, and humanitarian obligations. While a managed immigration policy can bring in needed skills and cultural diversity, the current approach often imposes hidden costs on citizens.

Pros:

- **Economic Growth:** Immigration can contribute to economic dynamism by filling labour shortages and increasing demand for goods and services.
- **Cultural Diversity:** A diverse society can foster innovation, creativity, and global connections, enriching the social fabric.

Cons:

- **Impact on Low-Wage Workers:** An influx of low-skilled labour can lead to increased competition for jobs, driving down wages and working conditions for domestic workers in specific sectors.
- **Pressure on Public Services:** Immigration can strain healthcare, education, housing, and social welfare systems. The costs of these strains are largely borne by local taxpayers, who may see reduced service quality or increased taxes.
- **Social Tensions:** Rapid or poorly managed immigration can

lead to social fragmentation and tensions, affecting social cohesion and trust within communities.

The question arises: are current immigration policies designed to benefit society as a whole, or are they being used as a tool to serve the interests of specific economic sectors and political agendas? Resources could instead be allocated to ensure that immigration policies are balanced, integrating newcomers effectively while safeguarding the interests of existing citizens.

Massive Government Spending: A Sustainable Path?

In recent years, governments have dramatically increased spending to stimulate the economy, support infrastructure, and provide social safety nets. While these efforts have been essential in times of crisis, such as the COVID-19 pandemic, there is a growing concern that this spending is neither sustainable nor equitable.

Pros:

- **Economic Stimulus:** Government spending can kickstart economic growth, create jobs, and support vulnerable populations in times of need.
- **Infrastructure Investment:** Spending on infrastructure can modernize a country's economy, improve productivity, and provide long-term benefits.

Cons:

- **Rising National Debt:** The massive spending spree has led to unprecedented levels of national debt, which future generations will have to repay through higher taxes or reduced public services.
- **Inefficient Allocation of Resources:** Poorly planned spending can lead to waste, corruption, and inefficiencies,

undermining the very objectives these policies are meant to achieve.

- **Opportunity Costs:** Every dollar spent on one program is a dollar not spent on another. There are significant opportunity costs when taxpayer money is directed towards programs that provide limited or unequal benefits rather than essential services like healthcare, education, or social welfare.

The Misuse of Taxpayer Revenues: A Call for Reprioritization

At the heart of these policies lies a fundamental question: are we, as a society, making the best use of our resources? The benefits of EVs, immigration, and massive government spending are often touted without a thorough examination of the broader implications. While these policies are not inherently bad, they are often implemented in ways that prioritize short-term gains or serve specific interests rather than focusing on more inclusive, long-term benefits for all citizens.

A Better Way Forward:

- **Reallocate Resources More Equitably:** Instead of pouring taxpayer money into subsidies for EVs that primarily benefit the wealthy, governments could invest in public transportation, renewable energy research, or community-based environmental initiatives.

- **Balance Immigration Policies:** Develop immigration policies that balance economic needs with social integration and cohesion, ensuring that the benefits are widely shared, and the strains are minimized.

- **Rethink Government Spending:** Prioritize spending that directly benefits the majority of its citizens, such as healthcare, education, and affordable housing, rather than blanket spending that may not yield equitable returns.

Conclusion

While the intentions behind policies promoting EVs, immigration, and massive spending may be well-meaning, the reality is that they often result in a misuse of taxpayer revenues that could be better deployed elsewhere. To truly serve the collective benefit of society, there must be a more nuanced, equitable, and sustainable approach to policymaking—one that genuinely considers who pays the price and who reaps the rewards.

Opinion: Big Tech Censorship and the Silencing of Conservative Voices

In recent years, the influence of big tech companies such as Facebook, Twitter (now X), Google, and YouTube has grown exponentially, shaping the way information is disseminated and consumed by the public. As private entities, these platforms possess considerable power over public discourse, wielding the authority to amplify or suppress content at will. However, a disconcerting pattern has emerged that raises questions about the ideological bias within these companies: the frequent targeting of conservative viewpoints for censorship, while often upholding government talking points and mainstream narratives in Western nations.

The Erosion of Free Speech in the Digital Public Square

Once heralded as bastions of free speech and open dialogue, major social media platforms have increasingly positioned themselves as arbiters of truth, deciding what is acceptable for public consumption. Ostensibly, their policies are designed to combat misinformation, hate speech, and harmful content. However, there is mounting evidence suggesting that these standards are selectively applied, disproportionately affecting conservative viewpoints and dissenting opinions that challenge prevailing governmental or mainstream narratives.

Consider the numerous instances where prominent conservative figures, independent journalists, and commentators have been de-platformed or shadow-banned. Whether it is questioning the efficacy of COVID-19 policies, critiquing immigration policies, or debating election integrity, many right-leaning voices find themselves under the microscope, facing suspensions or permanent bans. In contrast, more progressive viewpoints—even when controversial or potentially harmful—seem to be subjected to less scrutiny.

A Symbiotic Relationship with the State?

One of the most troubling aspects of this perceived bias is the apparent alignment between big tech companies and government interests, especially in Western democracies. During the COVID-19 pandemic, for example, social media platforms took unprecedented steps to regulate content that deviated from official government health guidelines, labelling dissenting perspectives as "misinformation." While some of these policies may have been motivated by public health concerns, they also set a precedent where big tech companies acted as unofficial enforcers of government policy.

In the United States, documents obtained through litigation and investigations have suggested that certain government agencies have been in communication with social media companies, urging them to suppress what they label as misinformation. The intertwining of government influence with corporate decision-making raises legitimate concerns about free speech, censorship, and the erosion of First Amendment rights in the digital age.

The Chilling Effect on Free Speech

The consequences of this perceived bias go beyond mere ideological inconvenience; they strike at the heart of democratic society's foundational principles. The marketplace of ideas thrives on diversity of thought and robust debate, allowing society to test and challenge ideas freely. However, when big tech companies disproportionately censor conservative viewpoints, they create an environment where certain ideas cannot compete on equal footing.

The chilling effect of such practices is profound. Content creators, journalists, and ordinary citizens may feel compelled to self-censor for fear of being de-platformed or losing their livelihood. This fear stifles creativity inhibits critical thinking, and ultimately weakens the democratic fabric by narrowing the range of acceptable discourse.

A Call for Transparency and Accountability

To be clear, tech companies are private entities with the legal right to enforce community standards on their platforms. However, given their outsized role in shaping public discourse, there is a compelling argument for increased transparency and accountability. Users have a right to understand how moderation decisions are made, who is making them, and whether there is an ideological bias at play.

Moreover, there is a growing need for a renewed commitment to the principles of free speech and open dialogue in the digital public square. If big tech companies are to maintain their role as arbiters of truth, they must do so in a manner that is fair, consistent, and free from political bias. The alternative is a future where public discourse is not determined by the merit of ideas but by the ideological preferences of a few Silicon Valley elites.

Conclusion

The power of big tech companies over modern communication and information dissemination is undeniable. However, the repeated targeting of conservative voices and the alignment with government talking points in the West raises serious concerns about the integrity of our democratic institutions. It is time for an inclusive discussion about the role of big tech in our society, the need for transparency in content moderation practices, and the importance of safeguarding free speech in the digital age. Without such scrutiny and reform, the threat of digital authoritarianism looms large, casting a long shadow over the future of open discourse and democracy itself.

Echoes of the Past: A Comparative Analysis of Contemporary Left-Leaning Governments, Immigration Policies, and Harold Wilson's Labour Era

In recent years, the rise of left-leaning governments in Western democracies, particularly in the United States, Canada, and the United Kingdom, has ignited fervent debate. Many have drawn parallels between today's policies and those of Harold Wilson's Labour government in the UK during the 1960s and 70s. The comparison is not merely academic; it serves as a warning, a historical echo of how well-intentioned, but ultimately flawed, policies can have long-lasting and devastating effects on a nation's economy, currency, social fabric—and now, national security, exacerbated by the destabilization caused by unchecked illegal immigration.

Harold Wilson's Labour Government: A Historical Perspective

Harold Wilson, who served as Prime Minister of the United Kingdom during two non-consecutive terms from 1964-1970 and 1974-1976, was, in his mind, a man of great political skill and intellect. His government was marked by a determination to modernize the British economy through extensive state intervention. This included the nationalization of key industries, such as coal, steel, and railways, which were seen as essential to the nation's infrastructure. Wilson's government believed that state control would lead to more efficient management and distribution of resources, fostering a more equitable society.

However, the reality was far different. The nationalization policies failed to deliver the promised economic benefits. Instead, they led to inefficiency, stagnation, and a bloated public sector. The coal industry, for example, became a symbol of decline rather than progress, as it struggled under the weight of bureaucratic management and lack of innovation. The steel industry fared no better, with massive government subsidies needed to keep it afloat, further straining the public finances.

Wilson's economic policies also had a profound impact on the British currency. The pound sterling was devalued in 1967 by 14.3% against the US dollar in an attempt to address the country's trade deficit and restore economic stability. However, this move, while necessary in the short term, undermined international confidence in the British economy and contributed to the persistent inflation that plagued the UK throughout the 1970s. By the time Wilson left office, Britain was teetering on the edge of bankruptcy, with the International Monetary Fund (IMF) stepping in to provide a bailout in 1976.

Contemporary Parallels: USA, Canada, and the UK

Fast forward to the present day, and the policies being implemented by left-leaning governments in the United States, Canada, and the United Kingdom bear a striking resemblance to Wilson's approach. In the United States, the Biden-Harris administration embarked on an ambitious agenda of expanded government spending, including massive infrastructure investments and social welfare programs. While these initiatives are aimed at addressing supposed inequality and modernizing the economy, they come with the risk of ballooning the national debt and overheating an already fragile economy emerging from the COVID epidemic.

Similarly, in Canada, Prime Minister Justin Trudeau's government has pursued policies of aggressive fiscal expansion, including significant increases in public spending on healthcare, education, and environmental initiatives. While these policies are popular with the electorate, they have raised concerns about the sustainability of Canada's public finances and the potential for long-term economic damage, particularly if inflationary pressures continue to rise.

In the United Kingdom, the Labour Party under Sir Keir Starmer has advocated for a return to higher public spending, particularly in the wake of the COVID-19 pandemic. Although the previous Conservative government had not fully embraced these policies, the political pressure to increase government intervention in the economy was palpable. The parallels to the Wilson era are clear: socialist policies risk exacerbating economic inefficiencies, increasing public debt, and ultimately leading to economic instability.

Orwellian Big Tech

As I reflect on the trajectory of Western governments and the behaviour of Big Tech leaders in recent years, I am struck by the alarming parallels to the dystopian narratives in George Orwell's seminal works, *1984* and *Animal Farm*. Both books serve as chilling warnings of authoritarianism, propaganda, and the erosion of individual freedoms—warnings that appear increasingly relevant in today's world.

Surveillance and Control: The Reality of Orwell's *1984*

Orwell's *1984* is often cited when discussing modern surveillance and control mechanisms, and for good reason. The novel presents a world where "Big Brother is watching you"—a society under constant surveillance by a totalitarian regime. In today's Western societies, we see a softer yet insidious form of this surveillance in the proliferation of mass data collection by both governments and tech giants. Edward Snowden's revelations about the extent of government surveillance programs, like the NSA's PRISM, show how Orwell's fiction has transformed into reality. The idea that "Nothing was your own except the few cubic centimetres inside your skull" resonates deeply in a world where privacy is increasingly elusive.

The tech companies, once viewed as liberating forces providing platforms for free expression, now wield immense power over public discourse. They act as the modern equivalent of Orwell's "Thought Police." Consider the way social media companies monitor, manipulate, and sometimes censor content under the guise of preventing misinformation or protecting public safety. While some regulation is undoubtedly necessary, the reality is that these companies often make opaque decisions without accountability, silencing dissenting voices and dictating the boundaries of acceptable thought. Orwell warned of this: "The Party told you to reject the evidence of your eyes and ears. It was their final, most essential command." Similarly, when social media platforms de-platform individuals or tweak algorithms to prioritize certain narratives, they are, in essence, controlling reality as the Party did in *1984.*

Language and Manipulation: Newspeak in the Modern World

Orwell's concept of "Newspeak," the language designed to diminish the range of thought, also finds its parallel in today's world. The manipulation of language to control public opinion is rampant. Euphemisms, jargon, and politically charged terms are employed to shape narratives. Take, for example, the terms "collateral damage" for civilian casualties in military operations or "enhanced interrogation techniques" for torture. These terms sanitize reality, making the unpalatable more palatable, just as Newspeak was designed to do. In Orwell's words, "War is peace. Freedom is slavery. Ignorance is strength." These paradoxical statements are disturbingly reminiscent of modern doublespeak that cloaks harmful actions in benign language.

Tech companies, too, engage in a form of Newspeak. The notion of "community standards" is often invoked to justify censorship, but whose community? And whose standards? When platforms like Facebook, Twitter, or YouTube ban content or de-platform users for violating these nebulous guidelines, they effectively control the range of permissible discourse. The result is a public that is increasingly conditioned to self-censor and conform, echoing Orwell's warning that "Power is in tearing human minds to pieces and putting them together again in new shapes of your choosing."

Power and Corruption: Lessons from *Animal Farm*

Orwell's *Animal Farm* offers a different but equally important lens through which to view the actions of Western governments and Big Tech. The allegory of a revolution betrayed—where once idealistic leaders become as oppressive as the tyrants they replaced—provides a stark warning about the corrupting influence of power.

"All animals are equal, but some animals are more equal than others," Orwell wrote in *Animal Farm*, capturing the hypocrisy of those who preach equality but practice elitism. This phrase can be applied to the current dynamics between Big Tech leaders and governments. For example, the revolving door between Silicon Valley and Washington, D.C., where tech executives frequently move into government roles and vice versa, raises concerns about who truly holds power. Is it the elected officials or the tech moguls with their billions of dollars and near-monopolistic control over information?

In Orwell's tale, the pigs who lead the rebellion against human farmers eventually become indistinguishable from those they overthrew, adopting the very behaviours they once condemned. In a similar vein, Western governments that champion freedom and democracy often engage in the same surveillance, manipulation, and censorship they criticize in authoritarian regimes. For example, the U.S. government's use of the PATRIOT Act to justify mass data collection on its citizens or the way European governments increasingly push for more control over online content, resemble the pigs' gradual slide into tyranny.

Divide and Rule: Creating Enemies to Maintain Power

In both *1984* and *Animal Farm*, creating external enemies or internal scapegoats is a tactic used to maintain control. In *1984*, the Party kept the population in a constant state of fear and hatred against perceived enemies, both foreign and domestic. Likewise, in today's world, we see governments and media outlets often engaging in fear-mongering, whether it's about immigrants, foreign adversaries, or domestic extremists. This fear is then used to justify greater control, more surveillance, and more draconian laws—often with the cooperation of Big Tech, which profits from stoking these divisions.

In *Animal Farm*, the scapegoating of Snowball becomes a way for the pigs to unify the other animals against a common enemy, diverting attention from their failings. Similarly, in modern politics, leaders often shift blame to foreign nations, political opponents, or marginalized groups, all while consolidating their power. It's a classic case of Orwellian distraction: keep the populace focused on manufactured enemies while eroding their freedoms from within.

Conclusion: Orwell's Warnings for the Present and Future

As I contemplate these parallels between Orwell's dystopian warnings and the contemporary state of Western governments and Big Tech, I cannot help but feel a sense of urgency. Orwell did not write his novels merely to entertain; he wrote them as warnings. His works are not just about totalitarianism in its most obvious, brutal forms, but also about the subtler forms of control that can take root in ostensibly free societies.

Today, we find ourselves at a crossroads. If we fail to recognize the dangers of unchecked government power, mass surveillance, the manipulation of language, and the concentration of power in the hands of a few tech elites, we risk sliding further into a world where Orwell's fiction becomes our reality. It is up to us to heed these warnings and to push back against the encroachment on our liberties—lest we wake up one day to find that Big Brother and the pigs have finally won.

Censorship

Further to my last post, I have noted the rise of Orwellian tendencies in media and governance in the West particularly in the UK, represents a deeply unsettling trend. This phenomenon, marked by the increasing suppression of free speech and the simultaneous neglect of pressing societal issues like illegal immigration, crime, and inflation, calls for a critical examination. One must ask: why has a society that once prided itself on its democratic values and the free exchange of ideas begun to resemble the very dystopian nightmares it once fought against?

George Orwell's "1984" serves as a cautionary tale against totalitarianism, where truth becomes malleable, and language is weaponized to control thought. The parallels between Orwell's fictional world and the current reality are striking. Today, governments, particularly those with left-leaning ideologies, are increasingly policing speech under the guise of combating hate. While the need to address genuine hate speech is undeniable, the criteria for what constitutes hate are often nebulous, subjective, and dangerously broad. This has led to situations where individuals are arrested or silenced for expressing views that challenge the prevailing orthodoxy.

The irony is palpable: in a supposed effort to create a more tolerant society, the freedom to express dissenting opinions is being eroded. This raises a crucial question: who defines what is hateful? When the state assumes the role of arbiter, the risk of ideological enforcement masquerading as public good becomes all too real. History has shown us that when governments control speech, it is not long before they begin to control thought itself.

At the same time, the focus on policing language detracts from addressing more tangible and pressing issues. Illegal immigration, rising crime rates, and rampant inflation are real problems that affect the everyday lives of citizens. Yet, these issues are often downplayed, if not outright ignored, by those in power. Why? Perhaps it is easier to regulate speech than to tackle the complex, and often politically inconvenient, realities that these problems present.

Mass illegal immigration, for instance, is a multifaceted issue that touches on economics, security, and national identity. However, discussing it openly often invites accusations of xenophobia or racism, further stifling honest debate. Similarly, rising crime rates and inflation are symptomatic of deeper societal dysfunctions that require serious policy interventions. Yet, addressing these issues would necessitate confronting uncomfortable truths about governance, economic policy, and social cohesion.

In this context, the media's role becomes particularly significant. Instead of holding power to account and fostering a platform for robust debate, many media outlets have become complicit in this Orwellian turn. By prioritizing narratives that align with certain ideological positions and by amplifying the policing of language over the discussion of substantive issues, the media is failing in its role as the fourth estate. This not only undermines public trust but also contributes to a culture of conformity, where deviation from the accepted narrative is punished rather than debated.

The question then becomes: why are we allowing this to happen? Why are we not more alarmed by the creeping authoritarianism that seeks to regulate thought and speech? Why do we tolerate the deliberate avoidance of serious issues that directly impact our lives?

The answer may lie in a combination of factors. The desire for social harmony, the fear of being ostracized, and the relentless pressure to conform to prevailing norms all play a part. But at what cost? If we continue down this path, we risk sacrificing the very freedoms that define a democratic society. The suppression of free speech, the neglect of pressing social issues, and the media's complicity in these trends are not just isolated problems; they are interlinked symptoms of a deeper malaise.

It is time to ask ourselves whether we are willing to accept this Orwellian reality, or whether we will demand a return to the principles of open debate, accountability, and the fearless pursuit of truth. The future of our society may well depend on the answer. So, remember these points next time you vote!

Reclaiming the Future—A Warning from Orwell

"Mandates, Motors, and Misinformation: A Critical Look at Urban Futures" has explored the complex realities of contemporary urban development, from the rise of smart cities to the rapid push for electric vehicles (EVs) and the often-misguided government mandates that shape these trends. Underlying these narratives is a more profound concern: the way governments and corporations, in the name of progress and sustainability, are quietly reshaping our cities and societies. George Orwell's works, especially *1984* and *Animal Farm*, provide a chillingly prescient warning of how unchecked power and propaganda can lead to controlled and manipulated futures. His vision is more relevant than ever in today's hyper-connected, data-driven world.

The Smart City Illusion: Technological Utopias or Orwellian Surveillance States?

Smart cities promise efficiency, sustainability, and enhanced quality of life through data and digital technologies. However, as explored in Part I, they also carry the risk of becoming surveillance states, where every move is tracked, analyzed, and controlled. Orwell's concept of Big Brother from *1984* looms large in the backdrop of these hyper-connected urban environments. The spectre of a society where "Big Data" replaces Big Brother, with a similar potential for invasive surveillance, social control, and erosion of personal freedoms, is not a distant dystopia—it is a possible future unfolding in real-time.

Orwell warned of the dangers of a state that knows too much, sees too much, and dictates too much. Today, the marriage of government oversight and corporate data monopolies raises significant concerns.

Algorithmic governance, touted as a path to more efficient urban management, can instead deepen social inequalities and embed systemic biases. Smart city initiatives, without adequate safeguards and democratic oversight, risk becoming instruments of digital colonialism and economic control. They can create homogenized urban experiences that stifle creativity, diversity, and the essence of what makes cities vibrant.

Electric Vehicles: The Promise of Green Mobility with Orwellian Consequences

The rise of electric vehicles, examined in Part II, is often portrayed as a triumph of green innovation. Yet, as Orwell's works remind us, what appears progressive on the surface can mask deeper problems. In *Animal Farm*, Orwell illustrated how noble ideals could be corrupted by power. The push for EVs, while ostensibly for the good of the environment, also exposes new forms of control and dependency. The control over rare earth materials, the centralized management of energy grids, and the imposition of top-down mandates can shift power dynamics in ways that prioritize corporate and state interests over individual freedoms and local communities.

Orwell's idea of "Newspeak," the deliberate manipulation of language to shape thought, is mirrored in modern narratives around green technology. The selective presentation of information, downplaying the environmental costs of battery production, the limits of recycling, and the strains on electrical grids, reflects a sanitized view that ignores the complexities and trade-offs involved. The Orwellian future is not just one of oppression by overt force, but also by subtle manipulation of truths—a warning for how we frame the discourse around EV adoption and sustainability.

Mandates and the New Propaganda: Navigating a Misleading Future

Part IV critically examines how mandates, whether for smart cities or electric vehicles, are often implemented without genuine public engagement or transparent debate. Orwell's insight into the dangers of propaganda—where governments manipulate truth to serve power—resonates in today's policy-making environments. Government mandates that ignore market realities, local needs, and public dissent risk fostering a new era of technocratic authoritarianism masked as progressivism.

The disconnect between governments and their electorates, explored in various sections of this book, mirrors the dynamics of Orwell's *Animal Farm*, where those in power dictate terms under the guise of public good, while the masses bear the consequences. The gap between public rhetoric and private reality creates fertile ground for misinformation and disillusionment, weakening the democratic fabric that should guide urban development.

Toward a New Urban Compact: Learning from Orwell's Warnings

In Part V, this book calls for a new urban compact—one that avoids the Orwellian traps of centralized control and misinformation. Instead, it must focus on decentralization, local empowerment, and the inclusion of diverse voices in shaping our urban futures. Sustainable urban growth should not come at the cost of privacy, equity, or democratic values. It must reject the Orwellian notion that some entities "are more equal than others" in dictating the shape of our cities and the lives of those within them.

Cities must be planned with transparency, human-centric design, and a commitment to ethical governance. Innovation must be balanced with caution, ensuring that technology serves to enhance human freedom and quality of life, not diminish it. The lessons from Orwell are clear: unchecked power, whether in the hands of the state or corporations, poses a threat to the freedoms and rights of individuals. Thus, the future of cities must be reclaimed by the people, for the people.

Charting an Open and Democratic Urban Future

As we stand on the brink of an uncertain future, we must heed Orwell's warnings against complacency. The urban futures of smart cities, electric vehicles, and government mandates are more than just policy decisions; they are reflections of power dynamics, governance models, and societal values. The path forward requires vigilance, critical thinking, and an unwavering commitment to democratic principles. Orwell taught us that the greatest threat is not just overt control but the manipulation of truth and consent.

To avoid the pitfalls of an Orwellian future, we must insist on open debates, transparent governance, and the right to question and shape our urban destinies. We must foster resilience not only in our infrastructures but also in our democratic institutions and social contracts. The future of our cities is not a distant dream; it is the outcome of our choices today. It is a future that must be built on a foundation of freedom, equity, and the unyielding defence of human dignity.

In a world of mandates, motors, and misinformation, let us ensure that Orwell's warnings are not our reality but a reminder to remain vigilant, informed, and empowered to shape a future that is not only smart and sustainable but also just and truly free.

Epilogue: The Road Ahead

As we stand on the brink of a new era defined by the promises of smart cities, electric vehicles, and sweeping government mandates, it is crucial to recognize that the future is not a monolithic destination, but a spectrum of possibilities shaped by the choices we make today. "Mandates, Motors, and Misinformation: A Critical Look at Urban Futures" has sought to peel back the layers of utopian rhetoric that often obscure the complexities underlying our ambitious visions for tomorrow.

The notion of progress has always been fraught with contradictions. On one hand, the potential for technology to enhance human life is immense; on the other, the rush to embrace the next big thing can lead us to overlook the nuanced, and sometimes uncomfortable, realities that accompany such advancements. It is easy to be captivated by the sleek narratives of tech-driven cities where sensors, AI, and electric vehicles seamlessly coalesce to create efficient, green, and livable environments. Yet, this vision, often marketed by those with vested interests, rarely accounts for the multifaceted and deeply human dimensions of urban life.

The idea of a "smart city" is compelling precisely because it taps into our collective desire for better living conditions, sustainability, and efficiency. However, we must be vigilant about the possibility of these cities evolving into landscapes where algorithms dictate daily life, where surveillance becomes ubiquitous, and where the social fabric is replaced by digital scaffolding. The balance between innovation and intrusion is delicate, and the decisions we make now will determine whether our cities become arenas of empowerment or encroachments on freedom.

The same critical eye must be turned toward the electric vehicle revolution. While EVs represent a significant leap toward reducing greenhouse gas emissions, they are not without their own ecological and social costs. The reliance on lithium, cobalt, and other rare earth minerals for battery production has already triggered geopolitical tensions and environmental degradation in mining regions. Moreover, as the shift toward electric mobility gains momentum, questions arise about the infrastructure needed to support it. Can our existing energy grids, many of which are outdated and overburdened, be adapted to meet this surge in demand? Or will we see new forms of inequality emerge, where access to clean and reliable energy becomes the dividing line between those who can afford the future and those left behind in the past?

The role of government mandates in this equation is equally complex. Policies designed to accelerate technological adoption and promote sustainability often come from a place of genuine intention, but they can also reflect a disconnect between lawmakers and the lived realities of the citizens they govern. A top-down approach may impose rigid frameworks on a landscape that requires flexibility, adaptability, and, above all, inclusivity. Without a deeper understanding of the socio-economic dynamics at play, well-meaning policies can inadvertently exacerbate existing inequalities, create new forms of exclusion, or foster resistance rather than cooperation.

This book does not pretend to have all the answers, nor does it seek to undermine the importance of pursuing a better future. Instead, it serves as a reminder that the pursuit of progress must be accompanied by a willingness to engage with its inherent complexities, contradictions, and challenges. We must be prepared to ask difficult questions, challenge dominant narratives, and remain vigilant against the unintended consequences of our actions.

As we forge ahead, let us remember that the future of our cities, our technologies, and our societies will not be determined by the grand promises of innovation alone, but by our commitment to ensuring that these advances serve the collective good. True progress lies not in the technology we build, but in the wisdom with which we choose to use it.

It is a road that requires careful navigation, open dialogue, and, above all, a recognition that the smartest city, the most advanced vehicle, and the most well-intentioned policy are only as good as the equity, sustainability, and humanity they help foster.

The road ahead is unwritten. It is up to us to decide which direction we will take.

Don't miss out!

Visit the website below and you can sign up to receive emails whenever John Shenton publishes a new book. There's no charge and no obligation.

https://books2read.com/r/B-A-RJUO-IATAF

BOOKS2READ

Connecting independent readers to independent writers.

Did you love *Mandates, Motors, and Misinformation*? Then you should read *Fried Chips*[1] by John Shenton!

2

In the modern era, the battlefield has evolved beyond the physical realm into a domain defined by data, circuits, and the unseen power of digital warfare. The chapters that follow explore a future in which the tools of destruction are no longer merely tanks, missiles, or infantry but algorithms, microchips, and covert sabotage. This book provides a thorough and sobering analysis of the challenges we face as we enter an age where wars are fought with lines of code, and the most valuable asset a nation holds is its technology.

A book about the effects of EMP, CME, sabotage, malicious code, etc in computer chips and integrated circuits as a means of hybrid warfare.

---

1. https://books2read.com/u/mlzqP7

2. https://books2read.com/u/mlzqP7

Also by John Shenton

Business Plan Basics
The Bahamas - More Islands and Recipes Than You Expect!
Collected Musings from Bricks and Mortar to E-commerce
The Smart City Odyssey: Unveiling the Secrets to Traveller-Centric
Software
The Dragon's Gambit: China's Bid for Global Dominance and the
Western Response
Silent Weapon
Business Basics: Money Sources
Influx
Fried Chips
Mandates, Motors, and Misinformation
Echos of Orwell
Control and Chaos
The Empire's Warning: What Rome's Fall Tells Us About the West
Today

About the Author

John Shenton was born in Birmingham, England and grew up in postwar England. He spent several years as a Radio Officer onboard a variety of vessels sailing to the Persian Gulf, the Indian Ocean and South China seas.

With degrees and a background in electronics and computers he has lived and worked within the United Kingdom, Germany, Switzerland and Canada.

While doing so, he established numerous trading relationships in Japan, Korea, the USA, China and other countries.

He has been retired for some time now living in Montréal Canada enjoying golfing, writing, sailing and many other things automotive.

About the Publisher

John Shenton published via Draft2digital